A Pedagogy of Poetry

IOEPress

Trentham
Books

For Sarah and Jem

A Pedagogy of Poetry
through the poems of W.B. Yeats

John Gordon

A Trentham Book
Institute of Education Press

First published in 2014 by the Institute of Education, University of London,
20 Bedford Way, London WC1H 0AL
www.ioe.ac.uk/ioepress

British Library Cataloguing in Publication Data:
A catalogue record for this publication is available from the British Library

ISBNs
978-1-85856-497-5 (paperback)
978-1-85856-597-2 (PDF eBook)
978-1-85856-598-9 (ePub eBook)
978-1-85856-599-6 (Kindle eBook)

Typeset by Quadrant Infotech (India) Pvt Ltd
Printed by CPI Group (UK) Ltd, Croydon CR0 4YY

Contents

Acknowledgements

Thanks to the pupils, teachers, and colleagues who have influenced this book. In particular, I thank the classes with whom I worked in the study of Yeats's poetry. Those who taught me have also shaped my thinking: Paul Jarvis (formerly my teacher of English at Wetherby High School), Tom Paulin, Mike Hayhoe, and Nigel Norris. I have also learnt much from English teaching colleagues, especially Doug Hackett, Sue Haynes, Sandy Cox, and Mary Gargett-Stringer. In my role as PGCE tutor, the comments and experiences of students help me develop my thinking. Thanks too to Morag Styles for encouraging my continued work in this area, and to Jeni Smith and Terry Haydn for their support.

Thanks to Jeffrey Wood for his memorable workshop, and to Lee for the psaltery birds. Sasha Matthewman's book lent me a perspective I hadn't previously considered. I am grateful for the permission granted by the National Library of Ireland to use their images in the chapter on 'Easter, 1916'.

About the author

Dr John Gordon is Course Director for the PGCE programme in English at the University of East Anglia, a long-recognized provider of outstanding teacher education. His doctoral study considered the pedagogy of poetry and children's responses to poetry they hear, and informed his innovative empirical research into teaching and learning around literature in the classroom. Dr Gordon is co-editor of *Preparing to Teach: Learning from experience*. He has published extensively in international journals such as *The Curriculum Journal, Changing English, English in Education, Educational Research*, and *Classroom Discourse*, and contributed a chapter to *Poetry and Childhood*, published by Trentham.

What is a pedagogy of poetry?

The ethos of this book

This book articulates the thinking teachers work through when they set about teaching poetry. It is largely unvoiced, tacit in practice, and difficult for the beginning teacher to access, other than through careful observation of experienced colleagues and personal trial and error in their own classrooms. I have sought to capture some of the thinking that can inform a pedagogy of poetry, and in such a way that teachers can find their own approaches suited to their students and the study texts before them.

For much of the last twenty years, poetry teaching has been low on the policy agenda for language and literacy teaching, so has not enjoyed significant research emphasis or funding. The last Ofsted report on poetry in schools (*Poetry in Schools: A survey of practice*, 2007) placed more emphasis on students writing poetry than on analysing poetry as literature in the secondary phase. Before that, the last publication of a government-sponsored document that attempted to describe effective practice in the literary study of poems was in the 1980s (HMI, 1987).

In the last decade or so, secondary school teachers of English have been subject to prescriptive frameworks that have determined the detail of their practice. Many of these, such as *The National Curriculum* (DfEE, 2000), outlined statutory obligations about what should be taught and even sometimes defined what sort of material might be suited to which age group. Further official structures, such as the *Secondary Framework for English*, conveyed not only details about the focus of learning but also guidance on how to teach: a centralized pedagogy. Concurrently web resources to support teaching have proliferated. It has become easy to acquire teaching resources and to find guidelines about the steps to take in teaching individual texts, often as ready-made lesson plans. From both directions, teaching has been shaped by tips and generic steps. Common principles have been applied across numerous subject disciplines, sometimes to the detriment of nuance.

I take the stance that though 'off the peg' resources and generalized strategies have their place, they cannot adequately prepare the teacher of literature for their work. Any teacher works with a unique group of students with their own dynamic, which comprises in turn individuals who will respond and communicate in their own particular way. The same can be said of literary texts: each one is unique, communicates in its own particular way, and offers its own distinctive voice. Indeed, that distinctiveness is part of its classification as literature – it is what takes it beyond the archetypal and generic. These two simple traits are crucial. When teaching literature, any approach has to take account of the individuals and dynamics in the immediate group of learners. Further, the teacher has to be alert to what is peculiar and special about the study text. Once these two elements – a unique group and a unique text – are brought together, there is bound to be a unique encounter that cannot be replicated in quite the same way. As with many public events such as a play in performance, a football match, or a music gig, something about the meeting will be intangible and unpredictable. Like these, each lesson needs an approach that moves beyond set routine or ritual, requiring some tailored application of expertise to make the most of immediate resources within the current circumstances. It is never the same twice.

For this reason, top tips and off the peg resources cannot be enough. Inevitably they circulate widely, because they are useful up to a point. They are swiftly absorbed and applied, and pragmatic use of available material is an essential skill for the modern teacher. Some aspects of professional expertise or action, however, are not easy to articulate in concise form. It is a little like the reality TV series, *Faking It*. Participants could take on a new role, such as that of chef or artist, and sustain the role for a few one-off events, but would be unlikely to fare well in the field for long without the subtle, developed knowledge and judgement that builds over time. Real expertise was not available to them instantly. I know through my own work that beginning teachers can see excellent practice and replicate it to good effect in their own teaching. It is a different matter entirely to develop a personal understanding of how to approach poetry or to refine judgement through experience about how to approach each new text and to present it successfully with various classes. Inevitably, new teachers sometimes make mistakes. These are a necessary part of the process of developing teacherly judgement, especially where a novice teacher is interrogating their own choices, their own rationale for their practice, and amending their work in response. At the same time, though, it can be useful to access the ways in which experienced teachers think. This book tries to convey some of the decisions and judgements they make as they prepare to teach poems as objects of literary study.

This does present a problem, however. For one thing, I do not want to present a top tips approach to teaching poetry, nor convey a single, monolithic or self-designating correct pedagogy for the field. Conversely, as soon as descriptions are presented in an applied context and become too specific to single texts, the principles may not be easily transferred to other works. Nevertheless, it is necessary to demonstrate the thought processes a teacher might go through, and this can only be done usefully if they are connected to illustrative examples.

I have tried to balance these matters by choosing to discuss teaching poetry with reference to the work of W.B. Yeats, but this is not a book about teaching Yeats's work alone. I chose Yeats because in my experience as a secondary-phase teacher of English, I found his poetry to be the most inherently complex and then the most challenging for pupils. That meant it was the most challenging poetry for me to teach, and needed the most careful consideration. It was hard enough to feel I understood it myself, but to support others towards understanding was another issue again. If this book succeeds in conveying the thinking that can inform teaching around his poems, the sorts of judgements described should be relevant to the challenges posed by other poems and poets. In short, I want to show how I arrived at my own method for teaching Yeats to help others arrive at their own bespoke pedagogies of poetry, whether for collections derived from single poets or for mixed anthologies. The poems used as examples here are poems I used myself in teaching, and were texts I had to approach with the demands of examination firmly in mind.

The audience for the book comprises any teacher of poetry, but given the focus on Yeats this will be especially relevant to colleagues working in the upper secondary phase. In the United Kingdom, that tends to cover the age range 14 to 16, post-compulsory education and early undergraduate teaching. I intend it to be of particular use to new teachers at each level. The discussions derive from my own early career teaching experiences, seared in the memory thanks to the effort and concentration Yeats required. They are shaped too, however, by my recent experience as a teacher-educator. My daily work entails supporting others towards independence as thoughtful, skilled teachers, attempting to draw together underlying principles with the sharp detail needed for effective classroom practice. At the same time, my role demands engagement with research specific to teaching and learning, and frequently this guides the discussions I have with colleagues of all levels of experience.

Accordingly, as this book is read chapter by chapter, frequent reference to educational research will be found. Some of it is well known and well established in teacher education and professional development, and applies across subjects and age groups. Other material is far more specific, intended for the interest of teachers of literature or literacy. Some of it derives from fields that are central to my own research enthusiasms, the first concerned with how young people learn through and respond to poetry. The second is focused on teacher knowledge and expertise, thinking through how each area develops and how they become manifest in the observable practice of teachers and evident in what they say about their teaching decisions.

The structure of the book

Each chapter has a focus around a teaching and learning issue relevant to literary study. The chapters outline thought processes that respond to the core issues, showing the judgements made relative to poems selected from the body of Yeats's work. The poems derive from a real selection, one that was prescribed according to the demands of an advanced-level specification. Using them here means that every point of discussion has its origin in classroom practice. The benefit of hindsight, further experience of teaching poetry, and later opportunity to engage fully with educational research means that I can articulate some aspects of the decisions I made with a thoroughness that I would have been unlikely to explain in such a way at the time. In a similar way, it is unlikely that beginning teachers will find their school-based colleagues have the time to explain their rationale for teaching at length, though their decisions will be the result of year-on-year of careful reflection, planning, preparation, and classroom dialogue: the knowledge that constitutes their professionalism.

In most instances the poems are provided in the chapters, so that it is possible to see the stimulus for each line of thinking and the decisions that follow, except for a few poems that are too long for presentation here. Being out of copyright, most of these can easily be found through web resources, though some editions of Yeats's work are referenced at the end of the volume after the chapters described below.

Chapter 1: Presenting poems: 'The Lake Isle of Innisfree'

The opening chapter reflects on the judgements teachers make even before students encounter a poem. How will that encounter take place and how will the poem be presented? Does it matter whether it is looked at in print, or if the group listen to it instead? I contend that the poem itself will often determine these choices: the teacher should decide which mode best suits its nature and take into account how presentation itself is bound to shape students' understanding of the text and the elements they come to consider most important. Further, this also becomes a matter of public and communal engagement with a poem, which is quite different from reading alone at home. The discussion develops to concentrate on presenting poetry in the aural mode, reflecting on the benefits and limitations of experiencing poetry as sound, where students listen to rather than see poems on the page. The potential of presenting the same poem in contrasting ways is explored. Through these various methods, students can additionally become very aware of how the encounter shapes their response, and can recognize how different modes direct them to interpretations within a related range. The chapter exploits the presentation of memory at work in the poem 'The Lake Isle of Innisfree' to consider how poems in general have the potential to act as mnemonic devices, machines for remembering, playing on our senses and directing our attention with subtlety yet also with sureness. In all of this, the chapter also considers making the most of the initial and relatively intuitive responses students might give to the poems they encounter before they are further mediated through questions and tasks.

Chapter 2: Poems as songs: 'The Song of Wandering Aengus'

Many poems have been adapted as lyrics for songs, while others explicitly present themselves as songs even though their first public presentation is in print within a poetry collection. Yeats's 'The Song of Wandering Aengus' is just such a text, with a clear signal offered in the title. This chapter reflects on the relationship between poetry and song, the distinctions and similarities between each, and how thinking about that relationship can guide the study of texts that position themselves on that boundary. It considers the use of poems set to music and how these can be exploited to help students understand individual texts, and for them to engage too with the question of where poems end and songs begin. Where is it helpful to use song versions of poems? Does it ever compromise attention to an authoritative printed text, or is such a view of page-based versions arbitrary and artificial? The chapter works from 'The Song of Wandering Aengus' and comments on versions set to music by Donovan and Jolie Holland, though the main thrust of discussion is to illustrate judgements about the use of each version and their part in a broader sequence. Later on, the chapter suggests the potential of drawing parallels between poems and songs in printed form, making a link between 'The Song of Wandering Aengus' and a popular song with its origins in the blues traditions of dustbowl America. Both embody the voice of a lonely troubadour seeking heightened experience, but is one any more poetic than the other?

John Gordon

Chapter 3: Poetry of place and nature: 'The Wild Swans at Coole'

This chapter considers a Yeats poem that has a firm correlation with a single location, 'The Wild Swans at Coole'. It reflects on how the places described can be made vivid to students through both the approach to the text and supporting resources. In addition, discussion explores the representation of places through poetry. To what extent can students begin to recognize the place-in-a-poem as a construction distinct from the location in actuality? Beyond attending to representation, the chapter introduces ecocritical approaches to literature. Both the location of Coole Park and the swans themselves provide a focus for demonstrating how a critical perspective can guide treatment of the text. However, the chapter seeks to illustrate how the teacher can draw from a range of perspectives concurrently rather than adhering dogmatically to one approach. Differing orientations to the text serve to highlight different features, consistent with the teacher's judgement of what deserves emphasis and how students' understanding might be developed in response. Along with all of the above, the discussion maintains close attention to the detail of the study text, ensuring that thinking about the poem in the context of critical approaches is always tied to the words of the source text.

Chapter 4: Finding a centre: 'The Second Coming'

'The centre cannot hold', a phrase in Yeats's 'The Second Coming', presents the challenge for the chapter and for teachers. How do we find ways to give students a cohesive, organized experience of a poem, to find a centre for the study in hand? This can be especially difficult with texts that are allusive, which contain multiple symbols, or which layer apparently unconnected images, all of which can be potentially bewildering to students. For the teacher, there are decisions about the degree to which they might take a didactic approach. Do they present their own interpretation or leave students to their own devices? The chapter describes a middle way, suggesting how to structure support so that students can develop their own insights. Still, this requires the teacher to formulate an interpretation, or at least to identify a range of valid interpretations, so that they can frame activity whereby students move towards thoughtful explanations of their own. In considering these challenges I draw on theoretical models of the reading process. These inform a view of how students, or any reader, can make sense of the text presented to them. Through conceptualizing these processes themselves, teachers can make an informed view about how to sequence and focus activities for students. This means that in addition to what they can observe or hear as evidence of engagement and response to a text, they also have means to influence private cognitive processes. They have a theory of reading and the likely intramental

6

processes their students are working through relative to the unique text for study, and use it to inform how they guide response to the text for attention.

Chapter 5: Making parallels: 'Sailing to Byzantium' and getting there

This chapter concerns the common literary activity of looking at two or more texts in juxtaposition, and additionally looking at form. Often poems presented as pairs, whether in class or in examination, are selected according to a common interest. Taking two Yeats poems about the ancient civilization of Byzantium, the chapter looks at the differing treatment of the city in 'Sailing to Byzantium' and 'Byzantium'. The difference in form between the two is evident in their contrasting lengths. The chapter considers the merits of looking at poems together, and the considerations behind their presentation. How can the sequence of presentation support understanding? The chapter considers how the texts can be used to develop understandings that are more than focused on individual texts, but which lead students to an appreciation of the development of a poet's craft over time. What constitutes development in poetic art? How is this demonstrated, and if it is identified, how can it be described? More than any of the poems considered so far in the book, these two, especially the second, are highly allusive. Many of their references will be unfamiliar to the young, casual reader. In reflecting on these aspects, the chapter also sets the foundations for those that follow which cover similarly allusive works, either as pairs or in isolation, due to their additional formal complexity.

Chapter 6: Head and heart: 'No Second Troy' and 'A Prayer for my Daughter'

So many poems portray individuals as their subject: Robert Browning's 'My Last Duchess', for instance, or, very differently, 'Timothy Winters' by Charles Causley. This chapter considers Yeats's portrait poems 'No Second Troy' and 'A Prayer for my Daughter'. The first was written about a friend, colleague, and unrequited love, Maud Gonne, while the second is self-explanatory. They both show us that portrait poems provide us with an embodied voice, a second persona beyond that of the subject of the poem. Frequently this voice will be construed as the direct voice of the poet, especially where the subject matter is as personal as it is here. The discussion looks at how each persona is created, and through looking at Yeats's very different poems shows how judgements about approach will differ accordingly. In addition, the chapter pays close attention to questioning technique, and how it can be possible to build from subjective, personal response to analytical attention to the craft of the poems. The orientation is linked to Bloom's taxonomy of learning, and is intended to support the development of tailored questioning according to a text-specific rationale.

Chapter 7: Poems of a moment: 'Easter, 1916'

A significant challenge for teachers of literary texts can be how to accommodate attention to the social, historical, and cultural contexts of their production. Inevitably this requires identification of relevant contextual detail, selection of items to be shared with students, and consideration of how these metatexts will be presented so that they enhance reading of the core text. How can we judge the balance of time spent on metatexts with the central poem? To what extent should the teacher direct students to detail, and for how long should they work independently to deduce relevance? Once the teacher has decided these things, there is the practical matter of deciding the teaching sequence and resources to be used. Yeats's 'Easter, 1916' is used as the source text, because it relates to an event of great importance in modern Irish history. Nevertheless, for readers a century later, the details may prove obscure. Circumstantial information not presented in the text may be necessary to support a reasonable level of comprehension. For the teacher, there is the question of students not only being party to this information but also engaging with it so that it enhances the intellectual and emotional understanding of the poem. How should metatexts be selected and presented, if they are not to prove a distraction from the core text for attention?

Chapter 8: Complex poems: 'Nineteen Hundred and Nineteen' and 'Meditations in Time of Civil War'

To anyone unfamiliar with Yeats's work, these are very challenging poems. They are far longer than any of the texts considered in previous chapters, and have complex formal structures that can be challenging to interpret. Like the Byzantium poems, they are highly allusive, though they use symbols and phrases that echo poems considered earlier in this book. The chapter suggests strategies to help students gain a foothold, some means of access to such difficult texts. These are related to conventional means, following a narrative or tracing themes or symbols, but using these poems as examples makes it clear how important the detail of the immediate poems might be to decision-making. Beyond each poem in isolation, the chapter begins to consider the impact of cumulative study, such that the swan symbolism of earlier poems has relevance to these later examples. Some of the activity here, especially about theme, requires the teacher to conceptualize ideas in the poetry in a way that will be both true to the texts and helpful to students. The teacher's own study and interpretation of the poems is clearly significant.

Chapter 9: Poems in sequence: Teaching an anthology

The last chapter of this book takes a different approach. While other chapters have been about approaching poems in isolation, or at most in pairs, Chapter 9 concerns the full collection of poems for study. It suggests ways of thinking about how to sequence teaching of a collection of poems. The decisions you make are likely to be guided by the nature and content of the poems, so generic principles for organizing teaching are unlikely to be appropriate. Though I use the Yeats poems discussed in the preceding chapters, my emphasis is on identifying the various principles for organization that could apply to any collection of poems and no matter who the poet may be. The same can apply to anthologies comprising the work of a variety of poets. Options include organizing the sequence according to the development of ideas in and across the poems; sequencing them according to the use of different and possibly increasingly complex forms; arranging them chronologically with attention to the poet's developing craft over time; or building students' responses step-by-step with corresponding attention to the terminology and distinct skills they can apply to each poem.

What may make each teaching sequence unique, however, is the possibility that the teacher may weigh each of these options and develop a sequence that takes account of each of these impulses concurrently. Developing a sequence for teaching thus entails exercising expertise and discernment, informed by a good knowledge of the students to be taught and their particular interests and needs for learning. With such an approach, each lesson will be integral to the success of the whole scheme, and learning will be cumulative. Though study of each poem will be prepared with great care, and to some extent be 'stand-alone', they will have a subtle role too in their purpose of providing a foundation for lessons to come or in referring back to earlier work. Overall, the sequence will have coherence and a structural integrity of its own.

The discussion in this chapter has some connection with the work of both Jerome Bruner (1966) and Robert Gagné (1970), who each reflected on the design of programmes of study and ways of looking at structuring learning in units that extend beyond individual lessons. Their ideas can only help the teacher of literature so far, however, when the texts for study also have a distinctive potential for pedagogy that also needs to be taken into account.

I have placed this chapter at the end of the book because the possible rationales for organization it describes are better understood once it is known what the earlier chapters contain and the principles they outline. In practice, the thought a teacher puts into sequencing their programme of study will usually take place prior to teaching, or as they begin to think about the opportunities individual poems present and how they can be exploited collectively. Once you are familiar with the book, this last discussion is probably the best place to start when you come to teach a sequence of poetry yourself.

Using the book

It is my hope that the advice you find in these pages can be applied to whatever poetry you may be teaching. I have used specific poems and the work of a particular poet to demonstrate how focused and in many instances how tailored the thoughtful preparation of poetry teaching will be. In doing so, my aim is to make evident the level of attention required for each poem and its distinctive qualities. When you align this with your knowledge of and empathy with your students, you will quickly move beyond the scope of my suggestions here. The process will no doubt lead you to further study resources, such as the distinctive metatexts that can inform your work around the study poems, and to bespoke material that is pitched to engage your students according to what you know to be their sphere of reference.

I hope very much that the process supports your own learning too. I titled this book *A Pedagogy of Poetry* using the indefinite article because I believe that there can be no one overarching or definitive approach to this area of literary study. Instead, there will be many distinct pedagogies developed by teachers as they balance their thinking about literary texts with their understanding of their students. From my own experience as a school teacher of secondary-phase English, and as a teacher-educator, I know that this absence of an easy, rule-driven strategy presents a key challenge for anyone beginning to teach literature. On one hand, it would be useful if there were clearly identifiable steps to take in planning your teaching of poetry. On the other, if the steps you take are too codified or generic you risk not only obscuring the unique and frequently rich character of your study texts, but also of diminishing what you might bring of your own expertise and personality to teaching. Try to bring these last two things to bear as you use the book.

There will be times – should be times – when the suggestions you find in these chapters do not apply fully, require some amendment or need to be used in a different order. If there is something you find here that leads you to think 'that doesn't work for my poem, or my students', but can articulate why it doesn't and what might make a useful alternative, you are developing your own pedagogy of poetry. For the most part, however, I want the book to be helpful, to provide a bridge between your early thinking about teaching poetry and early practice, and a step towards swiftly developing independence.

As you teach, you will apply expertise and have responsibility for the learning of others, but I believe that the path towards expert teaching is about your own sensitivity to opportunities for continued learning. In this I am influenced by the work of Amy Tsui, who asserts that:

> in the process of attaining and maintaining expert performance in all kinds of skills, experts engage in continuous efforts to improve themselves. Once they lose the characteristics outlined in the development of expertise, they cease to perform at an expert level; they cease to be an expert.
>
> (Tsui, 2005: 173)

Even if you teach the same group of poems in the same sequence twice over to two different groups of students, you will find the process very different. Responses will vary, as will the stumbling blocks and the moments of lucid understanding. Every time you teach is a learning experience for the teacher: you can't know how it will work out until you embark on the process.

Use this book in a complementary spirit, as a guiding framework for beginning to teach poetry. I hope that it gives you confidence in your work, that before long you will have several pedagogies of poetry in your repertoire, and that your students respond well to all of your teaching.

Chapter 1

Presenting poems: 'The Lake Isle of Innisfree'

Introduction

A common convention in the classroom study of poetry is to attend to poems as individual and discrete texts. When teachers begin to think about lessons in which a poem will be considered, they have in mind several matters. Of course these include reflection about the poem in question, but even at this apparently obvious level of preparation there are distinctions to be made. Will the focus be on establishing what the poem is about? Will it be necessary to identify and articulate a development of ideas or narrative across the poem? Is the poem considered because it typifies a given form and confirms its conventions, or is it instead an instance of form subverted? Are the ideas conveyed by the poem the central concern, rather than how it has been crafted, or is it essential to explore the relationship between the two? These represent just a handful of the choices that could be made, and indicate that even where we begin with thought about the text, we are concurrently drawn to making decisions about the purposes for using the poems in lessons.

Perhaps this can be summed up by thinking about the best preposition to describe the intended learning. If we say a lesson entails learning *about* a poem, this suggests being aware of detail beyond the text such as when and how it was produced. If we say learning *with* a poem this implies purposes beyond dealing with the text in hand, for example, engaging with a specific theme or idea, the poem selected as an apt resource and vehicle. Learning *through* a poem would be something else again, hinting at a poem as a distinctive means to experiential learning, and allowing the possibility that a chosen text can itself give rise to a unique experience, and hence learning, probably without recourse to deliberate and overt analysis. Is this learning through a poem quite the same thing as learning a poem, the preposition removed, or should this be interpreted as memorizing and reciting a poem for its own sake?

So far, we haven't even begun to think about the group of students who will engage with the poem, whether individually or collectively. What knowledge of learners and learning can a teacher draw on to inform decisions about how to engage students with texts generally, then with poetry specifically, and with the nature and demands of the chosen poem? On one hand, the lesson will encourage some engagement between the poem and each student as an individual, but this happens in the context of a collective experience, the fact that any lesson is a public and social event.

Accordingly, this chapter considers:

- Ways of thinking about poems to be used in teaching, as individual texts;
- Choices to be made about how a poem will be presented to students at the first point of encounter;
- The relationship between the chosen method of presentation and learning.

The poem used as a focus for the application of these principles

The text for attention in this chapter is Yeats's 'The Lake Isle of Innisfree', published in 1893 as part of a collection called *The Rose*. To Yeats's later irritation, captured in a 1930s recording (British Library, 2003), it became the most popular and widely known of his poems to the extent that for many it was the only poem they associated with him.

> **'The Lake Isle of Innisfree'**
> I will arise and go now, and go to Innisfree,
> And a small cabin build there, of clay and wattles made:
> Nine bean-rows will I have there, a hive for the honey-bee,
> And live alone in the bee-loud glade.
>
> And I shall have some peace there, for peace comes dropping slow,
> Dropping from the veils of the morning to where the cricket sings;
> There midnight's all a glimmer, and noon a purple glow,
> And evening full of the linnet's wings.
>
> I will arise and go now, for always night and day
> I hear lake water lapping with low sounds by the shore;
> While I stand on the roadway, or on the pavements grey,
> I hear it in the deep heart's core.

What a poem allows

The difficulties that arise from attempting to define what poetry is or how it works are testimony to the diversity of poetry and the many ways in which poems make and convey meaning. This is especially apparent with regard to the mode of poetry: some are experienced on the page, in the graphic mode, and some are experienced aurally, as sound. Even relative to this distinction, each mode allows and affords different forms of engagement. Looking at a poem on the page, a reader can often recognize the form of the poem prior to reading it word-by-word. This would be true of a sonnet, which Don Paterson describes as 'first and foremost: a small square poem' (Paterson, 1999: xii). An experienced reader of sonnets will anticipate some development of ideas across the octet and sestet, and expect some resolution of ideas in the final couplet. A reader encountering a sonnet for the first time will know that the poem is contained on the page and may take only a few minutes to read through: they can see the end.

This cannot be said of a heard poem, which unravels in time. On first hearing, no listener can know for sure how long it will be, and even if it conforms from the outset to the conventions of a familiar form (such as a limerick) it will not be clear until the whole text has been shared that the presentation is concluded and complete. A listener is given emphasis and rhythm by the performing voice, and multiple listeners hear the same. Working from the page, readers have to decode print and create a voice in their head, constructing emphasis and rhythm themselves, perhaps in their own voice (Attridge and Carper, 2003) or a reconstruction of the poet's voice, for example, the cadences of Simon Armitage heard previously on radio or audiobook. Similarly, a reader sees punctuation and line breaks, possibly noting emphasis or disjunctions relating to these, created by graphological resources not available to the oral poet.

Modes of communication in a far wider sense have been of interest to the education research community, the work of Gunther Kress and his colleagues pre-eminent. His work has considered how meaning is made and conveyed across different modes, and the implications of this for curricular detail and for pedagogy (Kress, 2003; Kress and Van Leeuwen, 2001). Most useful to us here is his term 'affordance' (Kress, 2003: 5), the capacity of any text to make meaning according to the modes of its composition. Certain ways of making meaning are afforded, some are not. A poem on the page uses several modes concurrently: graphological, spatial, semantic, syntactic, and that of the selected poetic form. It shares the semantic and syntactic modes with heard poetry, and so both can afford, for instance, the articulation of verbally expressed metaphors. A heard poem, however, cannot exist spatially, though it exploits its existence in the mode of time.

This concept of affordance is echoed in an idea called 'the pedagogical invitation', elaborated by Avner Segall (2004: 492) and which he applies specifically to texts used in school. Segall is not concerned specifically with literary texts but with the use of any text (for example, textbooks) in the school setting. He states that no text can be 'pedagogically innocent', but instead each text serves to 'create a world rather than simply re-present it' and is thus 'inherently pedagogical'. For Segall this means that separating how one teaches from what one teaches is impossible: 'a distinction between pedagogy and content is untenable'. The significance for teaching poetry is clear – that the poem becomes a central element of the chosen pedagogy from the very point at which students first encounter it.

Applying this thinking to a poem

How does the idea of affordance help us consider a poem for teaching, and what does it mean to consider a poem as a 'pedagogic device'? Consider the potential affordance of 'The Lake Isle of Innisfree'. The poem creates a world and makes the fact explicit, tracing the journey to Innisfree across the first stanzas yet revealing that this is a journey in the mind, the persona of the poem hearing 'lake water lapping … While I stand on the roadway, or on the pavements grey'. However, the poem complicates the relationship between real and imagined in the final line, which transmutes the insubstantial, internalized sound ('I hear it …') into a felt and physical experience at the root of being ('in the deep heart's core'). Sequence is a relevant mode: this path is experienced by both the reader of the page (visibly structured from one stanza to the next) and by the listener (revealed as heard in time).

Yet another significant resource is used. Within the verbal mode, the poem makes interesting use of verbs. That it should use verbs is not exceptional, though the range chosen is of note: I will arise, go now, go, build, made, will I have, live, shall have, comes, dropping, sings, I will arise, go now, I hear, I stand, I hear.

There are sixteen items here, and thirteen are different. In sequence they shift from verbs signalling intent and future action, to the present tense. They can be further subdivided into verbs describing states of physical activity (arise, go, build) and stillness (hear, stand).

Other word classes have a different effect. First, let us look at the noun phrases used:

Innisfree, small cabin, clay, wattles, nine bean rows, a hive for the honeybee, bee-loud glade, peace, peace, veils of the morning, the cricket, midnight, noon, purple glow, evening, linnet's wings, lake water, the shore, the roadway, the pavements grey, the deep heart's core.

These can be further categorized as concrete and abstract:

Concrete

small cabin, clay, wattles, nine bean-rows, a hive, bee-loud glade, the cricket, linnet's wings, lake water, the shore, the roadway, the pavements grey.

Abstract

peace, peace, veils of the morning, midnight, noon, purple glow, evening.

The items afford an emphasis on place and time, with most of the concrete nouns describing physical locations (cabin, glade, shore, roadway/pavements) and associated materials or features (clay, wattles, bean-rows, linnet's wings, lake water). In turn, they afford engagement such that the reader or listener may visualize settings and that tactile, textural qualities will be evoked. Of the abstract nouns, 'peace' is repeated twice, with the likelihood that the quality of peacefulness could become salient in the reader's impression. The noun phrases 'veils of the morning' and 'purple glow' suggest hazy, indistinct states, evoking a sense of softness consistent with 'peace'. Notably, the concrete nouns cluster in stanzas one and three, and the abstract nouns in the central stanza two, which is sequentially the poem's core.

On the page, the resource of stanzas supports the reader's sense of the journey from one phase to the next. This is not conveyed in different means through sound. Each spoken performance of the poem will be distinct and in this discussion I refer to a recording dating from 1933 of Yeats reading the poem himself (British Library, 2003). An immediate impression is that Yeats almost sings the poem. Certainly variation of pitch and shifts in emphasis are very apparent, thus the recorded text makes use of resources not available in print. The patterning provided by these resources draws the attention of listeners to specific details in an experience very different from reading the page. In this mode, repetition of the 'I will arise and go' refrain becomes significant as a structural and cohesive device, while patterns of assonance lend the poem a unity that cannot be experienced through the page. It is possible that the listener has a more immediate experience of the mood of the poem, manifest in tempo and the relationships between sounds.

Considering how our view of the text relates to our sense of the individual learner

It is commonplace now for learners to be described according to their learning styles, and for teachers to be aware of these, taking account of the work of

Howard Gardner which describes 'multiple intelligences' (Gardner, 2011). Gardner himself is eager that his conception of learning styles is not used as a blunt instrument attributing only one style to each student. Gardner believes that each of us has potential to deploy each of the styles he identifies, though we may have propensities and conscious preferences for some over others.

Poems tend to operate in several modes simultaneously and can thus appeal to several learning styles concurrently, though response and engagement may differ according to the learner's preferred style. All operate verbally, and thus largely appeal to the linguistic style, and this aspect of any poem as 'pedagogical device' is unavoidable. Beyond this, however, teachers can choose from a repertoire of activities and approaches designed to appeal to different learning styles. Frequently these are presented as generic 'teaching strategies' that float free of specific texts and even disciplines, so that they can be selected and applied to learning content at the discretion of the teacher. If we take Segall's point seriously, however, the text will suggest an appropriate strategy in that the nature of the poem will define the most useful means of presentation and consideration.

Semantically, 'The Lake Isle of Innisfree' buzzes with descriptions of sound, directs our attention to the action of hearing, and intrigues in the association of hearing with the heart. Regardless of whether it is presented in print or heard, the poem is transparently about hearing and in its play around the tenses it explores the relationship between sound and memory. Though any number of teaching approaches could support engagement with it, the poem suggests that an approach operating in the mode of sound will be especially apt. A complementary pedagogical strategy will therefore appeal to the aural learning style, so that the experience of the poem in the classroom provides space for students to reflect on hearing and memory as the two are evoked in learning activity. Whatever the poem to be studied, it should be possible for the teacher to identify an angle of approach influenced by the nature of the text. This does not have to relate to what the poem states through verbal means: a poem manipulating form and syntax in a way that draws attention (for example, making use of unusual line-breaks) is likely to support an approach interested in layout and graphology, and render it a priority before other orientations to the text.

Considering the presentation of the poem in the classroom

Louise Rosenblatt (1978) provides an appealing way of thinking about literary study in classroom settings, which she calls the 'poetic event'. She applies this term to any classroom encounter with literature, whether prose, drama or poetry, so it is possible she sees the poetry of the phenomenon in the whole encounter rather than the text alone. A 'poetic event' is the interplay of students, texts, and teacher in a classroom space, and it is only through this interplay that meaning is constructed. It is a way of looking at texts consistent with reader-response theory, which takes us beyond a focus on the meaning-potential of the text alone, and is implicit in what I have already described through reference to the affordance of texts. Rosenblatt's concept is presented in a tradition of literary theory, though it recognizes the distinctiveness of considering texts in classroom environments. It might be seen as the synthesis of literary theory with thinking sympathetic to the idea outlined by Lev Vygotsky (1986) that meaning and learning are negotiated and constructed between people through social activity and verbal communication, prior to individuals assimilating or settling on understanding that they might internalize. This line of thought is especially relevant to classroom activity based around listening to poems, which inevitably becomes a public and social experience due to the shared encounter with performances, whether recorded or recited. A lesson in which the core activity involves everyone listening to 'The Lake Isle of Innisfree' would constitute a unique poetic event, designed with coherence in mind.

A method taking into account the principles outlined

In this example, I seek to demonstrate how the approach to teaching the poem is complementary to the text itself. It is an attempt to use a method that relates to something distinctive about this poem, so the approach and its application will be unique to this text. That is not to say, however, that these principles could not apply to poetry teaching more generally. There is an underlying strategy that can be relevant to the study of all texts, to find an aspect or detail of the poem that shapes the pedagogy around which the lesson, or sequence of lessons, can cohere. The key detail in this poem is the concluding line, 'I hear it in the deep heart's core'. The line is salient in that it closes the poem, explaining how the imagined world of the isle also exists for the persona of the poem in the present, and inside him. It is a summation of all that has gone before: the poem as an exploration of the relationships between sense, memory, and feeling, with sound being the dominant sense. The classroom approach to be described echoes the same relationship, assuming it is also relevant to engagement with poetry as an institutionalized activity, the inevitable fact of classroom literary study. The dimension of feeling needs emphasis if we are to acknowledge the evocative potential of the poem and it is also required to avoid an overtly analytical, possibly dry orientation.

But is there really a division between analysis and feeling – or as Larkin would have it, the knife and fork – one taking apart, the other providing sustenance? To recognize the relationship between the two is important when teaching: if students don't get the chance to engage with the poem for its own sake and on its own terms, they are unlikely to develop any worthwhile response to the idea or experience embodied in it. The approach outlined here helps them, by degrees, to engage with and analyse the poem concurrently, working from a series of listening exercises. I owe a debt to Jeff Wood, co-author of *Cambridge Critical Workshop* (Wood and Wood, 1995), as the originator of this technique, which he applies to the study of Shakespeare's dramatic verse, specifically the soliloquies of *Hamlet* and *Henry V*. He has his students listening to a soliloquy and trying to note down what they remembered of it on their own. The emphasis on listening strikes me as very appropriate for 'The Lake Isle of Innisfree', and I decided to use it after experiences of reading the poem aloud to a class of 14-year-olds, who responded with sensitivity to its soporific rhythms and also articulated the 'sleepy' character of the poem. Their responses were not framed or guided, nor had we embarked on any discussion of the meaning of the text, through either paraphrase or analysis. It is relevant that they were a mixed-ability Year 9 class in a comprehensive school and that some of the comments were made by students with pronounced literacy difficulties and reading scores well below the national average. Seeing possibilities in listening activity, I honed a more deliberate approach for my future teaching around 'The Lake Isle of Innisfree', based on Wood's premise but adopting a more cyclical process.

The first stage is to share the poem with students. With 'The Lake Isle of Innisfree' I tend to use the 1933 recording of Yeats's performance, though because of its age the quality of the recording can obscure details. I persist in using it because of its atmospheric character, and because Yeats himself is speaking. His idiosyncratic intonation lends the poem an otherness that can intrigue students as much as it might at first put them off, so they need to hear it a few times to be able to tune in. Perhaps because of the lack of clarity, students are initially likely to struggle with the overt, semantic meaning and instead sense something of the mood of the poem and respond to its overall effect. I would recommend that for the first hearing students should be asked to put pens down, and simply listen. For this and further listening across the activity, they should have no access to the poem in print. Ideally they will hear the poem at least three times, as this is likely to have an impact on the quality of contribution in activities that follow. Once this initial phase of 'pure' listening is complete, ask students to take pen and paper and try, silently and on their own, to write down all they recall of the poem, however fragmentary that might be. At this stage they will need reassuring that it does not matter if they can commit only odd words and phrases to the page – half-remembered lines are fine. Similarly, it does not really matter if the sequence is not exactly consistent with what they heard: the point is to get as much of the poem on to paper as possible. It is an exercise in recollection, an initial note of what they think they have heard. It is wise to give them a time limit to promote urgency and focus. It can be valuable to ask the students which details were the first they noted down. Clearly these were some of the easiest to recollect, lodged in the memory with relative ease, and salient to the individual. For this reason the instances they share merit discussion: why were they memorable? The question at once forges the connection between intuitive response and analysis, requiring in answer some attention to the relationship between responses that are as unguarded as might be possible in a classroom situation, with the craft that triggered them. Students have tended to share many of the poem's concrete nouns at this stage, suggesting the stuff of this island home sticks in their minds. They occasionally recall phrases such as 'lake water lapping' or 'midnight's all a glimmer', suggesting that the sounds are important: the alliteration of the first or the balance of the 'm' and 'l' sounds in the second. These also give rise to comment about the poem's evocative imagery, and something further of the relationship between feeling and memory can be elicited: what pictures do they see in their mind's eye as they hear these, and on what experiences do they draw that are additional to what is provided in the poem?

Pedagogically, it seems logical that if students can collaborate with a partner they are likely to recover even more of the poem through their pooled resources. This should be done to a time limit, and if the teacher wishes there can be a further stage of sharing in a larger group, probably two pairs joining together to form a quartet. When it seems recalled details are exhausted the teacher can repeat discussion of the remembered items. Once students have a sense of what others remembered that they did not, does this affect their response? Do some students recollect images rather than patterns of sound, and others vice versa?

The next stage emphasizes sequence and requires students to transcribe the poem more deliberately, to render it in form on the page in whatever manner they consider complementary to the reading they have heard. This includes representing punctuation, line-breaks, and stanza divisions where appropriate. This is probably best done with a single scribe in each group writing the perceived poem on a large piece of paper (A3 or larger, to accommodate crossing out) or on a shared computer screen. Some students might have already started this process intuitively. You may feel that maintaining or reverting to pairs facilitates the concentration, precision, and quality of discussion they need at this stage. Monitoring pupil engagement and recollection from a teacher's perspective, I find such pair/group stages fascinating. Almost without exception items recalled with ease include most of the first stanza, though usually with some haziness around 'clay and wattles made'. This provides some insight into what students find unfamiliar – here the material of wattles, which therefore does not have resonance when heard, and so does not remain in the mind. Similarly, though something about a 'hive' is generally recalled, there is often discussion of the placing of 'bee', which some listeners believe to be combined with the former in 'beehive'.

In the second stanza, the metaphors 'dropping from the veils of the morning', 'midnight's all a glimmer', and 'noon a purple glow' tend to survive intact, though rarely are all three recollected by a single group. The first line of the stanza concerning 'peace' is less completely remembered, though its repetition leads to it being recollected in isolation. Of the third and final stanza, the last line is almost always remembered, as is the repetition of 'I will arise and go now', though 'night and day' and 'low sounds' are often lost. One or other of 'roadway' or 'pavement' survives, rarely both, though possibly the sense of being by some sort of road rather than the island idyll is what matters, and what Yeats intended we notice. He avoids repetition, which could otherwise distract from that final line.

In transcribing, students frequently form three stanzas consistent with the markers 'I will arise and go' and 'And I will have some peace there', which are also heard. Line length seems harder to gauge, with the longer lines in the second stanza sometimes halved to form two. The end result is that students often manage to transcribe most of the poem, and this in itself can surprise them as they expect neither their memories to serve them so well, nor a poem to function so well as a 'mnemonic aid' (Ong, 1982: 35). In the concluding phases it then becomes possible to consider the power of listening ostensibly as it relates to the activity: what is the relationship between listening and recollection? When asked this, students tend to make the connection with the experience of the persona of the poem too, that he recollects a rich world of images and particularly of sound.

Having considered the way in which aspects of the poem can manipulate attention and to varying degrees support the listener in holding on to details as well as gaining an underlying sense of the feel of the poem, the listening and transcribing activities can aid consideration more akin to conventional analysis. But the analytical work that follows derives from these early stages of engagement, and is not separate. Students can be invited to explain why they believe their decisions about the formatting of the poem are legitimate (not 'correct' – this is not about reproducing the form exactly as found in the original). This can be explored through whole-class discussion, though much can be gained through one pair or group joining with another to compare their formatting. Most importantly, they should articulate why they have separated stanzas as they have, and comment on their choices of punctuation and line-breaking. These thoughts again often have the effect of returning attention to the heard performance, and reveal the impact of silences and their variation. Concurrently, students are also led to consider the organization of ideas, whether at line or stanza level.

The work can be concluded in several ways. One can simply reveal a printed version of the text and invite comment on what the most surprising feature of this mode might be relative to what has been heard and their own transcribed versions. This can be taken a step further by presenting an alternative draft, such as the one provided in the biography of Yeats by Richard Ellmann:

> I will arise and go now and go to the island of Innis free
> And live in a dwelling of wattles – of woven wattles and wood
> work made,
> Nine bean rows will I have there, a yellow hive for the honey bee
> And this old care shall fade.
>
> There from the dawn above me peace will come dropping
> down slow
> Dropping from the veils of the morning to where the household
> cricket sings.
> And noontide there be all a glimmer, midnight be a purple glow,
> And evening full of the linnets wings.

(Ellmann, 1964: 124)

Copies could be deployed to afford consideration of form, one obvious feature being that this concludes in only two stanzas rather than three. Why and how does this affect the development of feeling and ideas when compared with the published version?

Presenting the poem aloud can also be valuable, perhaps around an open question such as *Which phrases most interest you?* If necessary this can be refined: *Which are interesting insofar as they are either preferable to or less effective than the final version as performed by Yeats?* I have heard students remark that 'a dwelling of wattles – of woven wattles and wood work made' overdoes the alliteration such that it becomes distracting. The line 'And this old care shall fade' is considered rather too direct, while the layer of the poem concerned with memory is not so prominent in this version. In lacking a third stanza the draft misses the framing device from the perspective of the 'pavement grey', as it also lacks a resonant and summative line with the appeal of 'I hear it in the deep heart's core'.

Another possibility is to share with students an alternative recording of the final version, or even have one half of the class work with the Yeats reading and the other with the second recording. If both work through the processes outlined above it becomes possible, through ultimate comparison via plenary work, to consider the extent to which it is the performing voice or the substance of the poem that most affects response and influences the workings of memory.

Conclusion

Though I have used 'The Lake Isle of Innisfree' as the poem for attention, the approaches and principles can be generalized and applied to other poems, with the teacher reflecting on any or all of the following:

- Informing the chosen approach with something inherent and distinctive to the poem;
- Recognizing the affordance of the poem and the impact the mode of presentation used in the lesson can have on students' responses and interpretations of the text;
- The interplay of the public, shared encounter with the poem and individual response;
- The role and power of memory;
- Supporting concentrated and attentive listening;
- The role of sound-features;
- The possibilities of experiencing poems away from print;
- The juxtaposition of different recordings and drafts of the same text as a way of noticing features of the core text;
- Developing activity and thought through cumulative tasks, starting with individuals and shifting to pairs and larger groups where appropriate.

Most important of all is the pedagogical principle of developing an approach where the mode of teaching is consistent with the nature of the text, such that the lesson is coherent and crafted with a unique internal logic of its own, just like a poem. It is possible to describe what happens as both 'learning the poem' and 'learning through the poem', with almost all response and discussion generated from the encounter with the text as a heard performance.

Chapter 2

Poems as songs: 'The Song of Wandering Aengus'

Introduction

The poem 'The Song of Wandering Aengus' has been adopted by numerous performers and is frequently set to music in contemporary recordings, since even the title marks the text as a song. A quick search of audio files available through an online marketplace or YouTube yields over forty versions, a fair number presented by acts working in the genre of Irish folk music. There are examples too by long-standing and high-profile performers: a version by Donovan from 1970, another by David Gray singing live in 2009.

It is not unusual to find musicians interpreting poetry in this way, whether or not the poet declared the original work a song. In the 1990s Yeats's work was the subject of a collection called *Now and in time to be*, which featured Van Morrison, Christy Moore, Shane McGowan, and The Cranberries singing versions of his poems. Other collections by single acts include *Yeats is Greats* (sic) by The Speakers, a lo-fi Americana appreciation mixed with their own songs, and more recently *An Appointment with Mr Yeats* by The Waterboys (who also recorded 'The Stolen Child'). Gerard Manley Hopkins has been similarly honoured by Sean O'Leary, while American vocalist Josephine Foster recorded an entire album of Emily Dickinson poems. Poets themselves have put other poets to music, Allan Ginsberg's versions of William Blake's poems set to the hurdy-gurdy being a memorable example. Carla Bruni, former French First Lady, released an album interpreting canonical poetry and including Yeats's 'Before the World was Made' and 'Those Dancing Days are Gone', alongside poems by W.H. Auden and Dorothy Parker.

This chapter considers Yeats's poem and recorded song versions with the following general questions in mind:

> *For what reasons might teachers use song versions of poems with classes?*
> *What might be significant or useful about the relationship between a printed poem and a rendering of it as a recorded song?*

*Where two or more recorded interpretations exist, how can
they be used?*
*What informs a teacher's judgement about a good balance between
attention to the source text and recorded versions? Does it matter?*
*What can be said of the relationship between poetry and song that
can inform the teaching of poetry, and how if at all should the
distinction between the two be made?*

The poem

The poem was first published in 1899 as part of the collection *The Wind
Among the Reeds.*

'The Song of Wandering Aengus'

I went out to the hazel wood,
Because a fire was in my head,
And cut and peeled a hazel wand,
And hooked a berry to a thread;
And when white moths were on the wing,
And moth-like stars were flickering out,
I dropped the berry in a stream
And caught a little silver trout.

When I had laid it on the floor
I went to blow the fire aflame,
But something rustled on the floor,
And some one called me by my name:
It had become a glimmering girl
With apple blossom in her hair
Who called me by my name and ran
And faded through the brightening air.

Though I am old with wandering
Through hollow lands and hilly lands,
I will find out where she has gone,
And kiss her lips and take her hands;
And walk among long dappled grass,
And pluck till time and times are done
The silver apples of the moon,
The golden apples of the sun.

Song versions for discussion

I refer to two versions of the poem in this discussion, one by Donovan (1970) and one by Jolie Holland (2006).

Donovan will for many be the better known performer, famed and caricatured in the sixties as a British counterpart to Dylan by virtue of his folk-oriented sound. Compared to Dylan, however, his influences were more overtly psychedelic, as some of his song titles and record sleeves attest. Released as the B-side to a seven-inch vinyl single, his version of 'The Song of Wandering Aengus' is not one of his best-known releases, though resurgent interest in Donovan and YouTube preserve the track's availability for a still substantial audience. The track itself is a relatively straightforward interpretation in the folk genre: Donovan as lone troubadour with guitar, tremulous voice, and little more.

Jolie Holland's version, by contrast, is a more recent recording with a fuller arrangement, recalling at times the rich evening mood of Jeff Buckley's album *Grace*. Her voice has been likened to Billie Holliday's, and her music is often discussed as an example of American folk blues. The track can be found on her album *Catalpa*. 'Catalpa' refers to a deciduous species of tree which can be used as tonewood for guitars. Perhaps Holland intended a resonance with the hazel wand? Yeats also mentions the catalpa tree in his poem 'The New Faces', published in 1928.

Clearly there is no substitute for listening to the tracks before reading my discussion of their use, so I recommend you find the audio tracks on CD or the web. Some suggested links are provided at the end of this chapter.

The benefits of hearing the song

Whenever I present a poem to students, I want them to engage with it as far as possible on its own terms, to respond to the poem with some immediacy, some intuitiveness, prior to analytic thought. That can be difficult in classrooms, where students come to know the game and are aware of a broader assessment framework. More to the point, they may not be approaching a poem like this out of choice. When I think about how the poem engages listeners or readers I note that the economy of the narrative is striking. A related secondary trait is its first-person voice. We can recognize these characteristics as common to songs too. If I try to reduce the purpose of my students' engagement with this poem to its simplest level, it is that I want them to recognize and respond to it first as a story. Their response could be to what happens, or it could be to the voice telling the story, and thus to a person. Both permit a fairly immediate reaction.

The availability of recorded versions allows me to foreground both the narrative aspects and the presence of a narrating voice. Working with a recorded version before seeing the poem in print means students can experience the text as a developing story, becoming subject to its hooks and surprises in the moment. Unlike an encounter on the page there is no possibility of taking in details to come, however inadvertently, through glances down or across a page. It is also possible that the effort of listening supports attention to the detail of the text in a manner distinct from reading from a book. For some students this will seem a more relaxed encounter, easier than reading print.

The matter of access to the narrative inevitably influences the teacher's selection of recorded texts. Assuming only the Donovan and Holland resources are available, which is likely to promote the best initial grasp of narrative detail? My own feeling is that it is the Donovan version, first, because it has the simplest arrangement, and second, because the voice is clearest. Third, I find Donovan's diction very precise: it is easy to hear the words. Nevertheless, I make the selection knowing that these reactions to voice are subjective. Students might relate differently to the two singers according to their own gender, for example. Because the protagonist of the poem's narrative is male, it is an important teaching point for me that I do not obscure that fact. If the name Aengus is not familiar to pupils as male, the Donovan version can gently underline the fact.

The relationship between poetry and song

To teach any poem that declares itself as a song, or a poem that is set to music, is to invite consideration of the distinction between songs and poems. How do we differentiate between the forms? If you choose to explore this matter, you inevitably come to delineate the characteristics of poem and song more precisely. In the endeavour of learning through literary study, the opportunity to reflect on the nature of poetry can support students in their developing capacity to describe texts and their unique means of communicating. Within a course, this can be helpful in guiding their appreciation of the differing presentational strategies, working and effects of novels, poetry, and drama scripts: each form has its unique relationship with readers, listeners, or audiences. This is about teaching poetry as poetry – a way of conceiving the form that is not directly interchangeable with other types of literary texts and associated modes of engagement.

Perhaps the most simple, commonplace understanding of a song is words set to music. Yet even this usually supposes words with some form of internal patterning that survives even where the musical setting is removed. In form, then, the verbal element of songs will probably be patterned with end-rhyme or a consistent rhythm. Even so, as poet Michael Rosen observes, in a song it is possible for words to 'get away with supporting themselves with a melody', so we tolerate the words 'I love you' in songs though they are so clichéd and familiar. Poems, he notes, 'can't usually get away with that repetition and ordinariness' (Rosen, 2007). General readers agree:

> A good song is one in which the listener can hear and understand every word, can follow the story, and can respond, either by singing a chorus or by humming the melody. And it must do all these things the first time you hear it.
>
> (Wallace, 2013)

Other understandings of 'song' relate less to its formal qualities than to its effect: 'a term used broadly to refer to verbal utterance that is musically expressive of emotion' or 'for literary purposes … personal utterance projecting a limited emotional stance experienced by a single person'. When poems use the term 'song', and where they have been created without attention to accompanying music, a relationship with music can only be implied. This may comprise some of the formal qualities suggested above, or in semantic features that convey a tone or mood. Words may be used not only to state or represent directly. Vocabulary may be selected, combined, and accumulated to evoke certain feelings or impressions. Let us call these examples 'songpoems' and accept 'The Song of Wandering Aengus' into that category.

Approaching a songpoem

Before teaching a songpoem it is useful for the teacher to identify the characteristics of the text that echo the definitions above. What is its own unique combination of these elements? Let's look again at the opening stanza of 'The Song of Wandering Aengus':

> I went out to the hazel wood,
> Because a fire was in my head,
> And cut and peeled a hazel wand,
> And hooked a berry to a thread;
> And when white moths were on the wing,
> And moth-like stars were flickering out,
> I dropped the berry in a stream
> And caught a little silver trout.

Clearly the song is uttered by an individual and describes their experience. This first stanza has narrative momentum too, outlining a sequence of events with little figurative decoration. Much of the vocabulary is monosyllabic, and has a quite limited range. Of its 55 words, *hazel*, *berry*, and *moth/s* are each repeated twice, and only 37 different words are used in total. The nouns are concrete and their modifiers derive from nouns (*hazel* and *moth-like*). Many of the verbs used correlate with concrete nouns too: *cut*, *peel*, *drop*, and *hook*. It has a simple and recognizable, if not entirely consistent, rhyme scheme of *abab* with half-rhymes on the a-rhyme. *Head/thread* and *out/ trout* are complete, but *wood/wand* share only their consonant sounds while *wing/stream* is a very loose echo indeed. The metre too is very regular, which becomes quite obvious if you try to utter it as a military marching song.

In summary, the text is identifiable as a song even if the title is removed. It would be reasonable to expect that if listeners heard it first as a song to music, they would accept it as such. If, however, and according to the definitions above, the words in poetry do something more subtle and sophisticated than words in songs, we can allow for the possibility that some qualities will reside in the words that distinguish them from prose, whatever the manner of their presentation.

Presenting the songs in the classroom: overview

Imagine then that I work with 'The Song of Wandering Aengus' in the classroom, presenting it first as a song set to music. Though I use this poem as the point of departure, the process outlined could apply to any comparison of differing recorded versions of a single printed poem.

I will include the following in my lesson elements, in this sequence:

1. Share with students the recorded version of the song put to music by Donovan.

2. Discuss the Donovan version on its own terms, with an emphasis on initial engagement and comprehension of narrative and character.

3. Share with pupils a second recorded version, this time Jolie Holland's.

4. Discuss the differences between the two presentations, first emphasizing the general effect on listeners and then the feelings and mood evoked by each.

5. Consider the poem in print, attending to details foregrounded by versions of the poem set to music.

6. Evaluate the extent to which 'The Song of Wandering Aengus' belies its title in having characteristics that are attributed to poetry, this time with reference to a third recorded song called 'The Big Rock Candy

Mountains'. This stage will also trace distinctions between songs and poems, both personal and established in literary criticism.

Presenting the songs in the classroom, step by step

Stage one: listening to the first recorded version
This activity assumes the relative clarity of Donovan's diction and hence the transparency of the narrative. Nevertheless I would play the recording through at least twice. The initial listening should be undirected, so students can hear it for its own sake, naturally and unmediated as far as is possible in a classroom setting.

Stage two: developing response to the first version
For further listening I would provide students with prompts. I might indicate that I would like students to listen with particular attention to the story in the song, and after playing it ask students to note down all they remembered, transcribing words, phrases, and half-recalled fragments. A further step would be to ask them to discuss their notes with their neighbour, checking for detail and chronological accuracy through cross-reference and shared memory. This could involve more than one extra hearing, or hearings interrupted with a pause after each stanza. The nuanced choice here will be down to the individual teacher's judgement of what is apt for their poem and what is suited to their class. Then ask students to share their responses further, either in new and larger groups (of four or six?) or as a whole-class plenary, to arrive at a consensus about the narrative.

Stage three: hearing a second version
As with the first experience of the Donovan version, the initial encounter with Holland's version should be unmediated. The approach students have to this cannot be as innocent, because they already have knowledge of the narrative which is by now more thoroughly assimilated and has been subject to shared discussion. It is likely that whether or not this version is signalled overtly for comparison, students will orientate to responses that are relative to their encounter with the Donovan version.

Stage four: attending to differences
Because the narrative is already established, there is no need to elicit it again with the second poem. Instead, the questioning aims to guide students to reflect on the differing presentational characteristics of each version. If there is a distinction (and the two versions have been selected because I feel they evoke contrasting moods) this may be experienced by listeners through

differing play on their emotions. Even where listeners feel relatively unmoved by both, they can offer a response about which version best matches their understanding of the story. Questions that have an affective focus could include *Which of the two versions of the song affected you most, and why?* or *Did the versions have differing effects on you?* Or more directly: *Which did you prefer?* though this can elicit an emphasis on personal tastes in music rather than textual detail, so follow-up questioning is needed to refocus attention to the texts for study. This can be achieved through questions about the suitability of singing styles and music to the narrative, or about which of the recordings best evokes the right mood in the view of students. Whatever the choice of question around preference, it needs to lead towards attention to style or emotional effect.

Remember that at this stage we are yet to see the song in print, so comparative work may benefit from renewed attention to the recorded versions, played in quick succession. The principle of selection can be applied here and to any paired texts, isolating stanzas where the differences in presentation are most evident. I would select the final stanza for one simple reason: I expect the last stanza and its detail to be the one students are likely to be least secure with. This is purely a matter of text sequence and memory, as listeners tend to find it easiest to concentrate on the initial stanzas that provide establishing details by way of exposition.

My second purpose is to mark the distinction between these two versions, and there are marked differences in both vocal aspects and musical character. Donovan keeps to a regular rhythm with consistent and stark guitar accompaniment, and similarly sings in a fairly consistent narrow range of pitch and volume. Holland's version for me conveys more warmth and emotional engagement on behalf of its voice, that of Aengus, and it has a more upbeat rhythm. I comment further on these distinctions in a moment. A final reason for selecting this stanza for attention is to dwell on it so that the shift in narrative perspective is noted. It is a crucial shift in the poem, indicating that Aengus still wanders in search of the glimmering girl, apparently into his old age, and that he will do so tirelessly until she is found. If I wished to approach the poem in a traditional manner, concern with its themes, memory, age, and the passing of time would be especially relevant. Through this approach I create an environment where there is the possibility of reaching the same themes laterally, through guided engagement.

A juxtaposition of versions like this marks differences in presentation, and both musical and verbal distinctions mark different details of the song for attention. The annotated stanzas below, one for each version, show some of the aspects of performance that I noticed, described in an informal vocabulary rather than a specialist jargon of musical commentary. The italics signal the details remarked on in the further notes.

The Donovan version

Though I am old with wandering	
Through *hollow lands and hilly lands*,	emphasis on alliteration and partial repetition
I will find ou*t* where she has gone,	mannered emphasis on 't' in 'out'
And kiss her lips and *take* her hands;	emphatic 'take'
And walk among long dappled gra*ss*,	mannered susurration of grass
And pluck *till time and times* are done	alliteration very apparent
The silver apples of the moo*n*,	prolonged 'n' sound
The golden apples of the su*n*.	prolonged 'n' sound

The stanza is set to a regular guitar accompaniment that only changes after the singing concludes, descending, as if winding down. This is soon combined with a plaintive keening that initially sounds like an oboe, but is Donovan's voice. This becomes more obvious as it increases in definition as a verbal utterance, something akin to 'away' but still not entirely clear.

The Jolie Holland version

In this version there is a lengthy instrumental interlude between stanza two and the final one. The musical arrangement is fuller and more layered: in addition to a rhythm provided by acoustic guitar there is a less regular, tremulous guitar sound that varies in volume and emphasis. This sounds a little more impressionistic, evoking a warm evening. Richie Haven's version uses a similar sound and offers an alternative for similar effect. The first four lines have a steady musical pattern, though the accompaniment changes to acoustic guitar alone on line 5, while becoming more upbeat. After Holland completes her singing, a simple guitar figure ends the recording.

Though I am *old* with *wandering*	Old and wandering prominent
Through *hollow lands and hilly lands*,	Like Donovan, the alliterative phrase is stressed
I will *find out where* she has *gone*,	Entire line: shifts to more histrionic vocal style
And kiss her *lips* and take her *hands*;	Nouns stressed and prolonged
And walk [among long] dappled grass,	'among long' changed to 'along warm'
And *pluck* till time and times are *done*	Verbs stressed

The silver apples of the moon,
[and] The golden apples of the sun.   'And' added at start of line

How would I approach treatment of these features in my teaching? Probably by providing students with two blank copies of the final stanza, each double-spaced and with surrounding white space to allow for annotations during at least two hearings of the isolated and juxtaposed extracts. The easiest starting point is to ask what appears different, categorizing according to distinctions of music and singing.

In terms of pedagogy, my own comparison and annotations prior to teaching are important. That is when I realize that the distinctions in utterance may signal something about the character of the voice in relation to the events they describe. Why, for example, is 'I will find out where she has gone' so different in the Holland rendition? What does this tell us about her version of Aengus? (I would suggest a combination of his yearning and determination, and the overwhelming power of both.) Donovan's singing draws attention to alliterative phrases and hence to patterning of sound in the song. The modification Holland makes to include 'warm' is interesting too. Combined with the swifter end to the music in her version, emphasis on the couplet, where elements are tied with 'and', hints that Aengus finds the girl and an idyll with her, at least in the imagination, through the reverie of the song itself. In sum, her version seems to suggest a satisfying closure. Donovan's version of the song does not allow the singing Aengus to bring the text to an end with the words: there is an epilogue of sorts which suggests far more anguish than Holland's interpretation. This Aengus seems still to be wandering, his song echoing unrequited through hollow lands.

Stage five: back to poetry
The juxtaposition of two carefully selected extracts of recorded songs draws attention to textual detail, and foregrounds the potential for interpretation given the different new texts that emerge. Where multiple versions of a poem exist, the teacher can select versions according to the interpretations they afford both individually and in contrast. At the same time points of similarity emerge: for example, that both versions here seem to slow and to stress 'through hollow lands and hilly lands', suggesting a quality within the words that remains no matter the chosen intonation. The poetry is inherent regardless of the musical setting. The teacher can plan to seek student opinion as to why this is so. I would ask students to attend to the sounds of the words in combination and their impact on fluency. The frequency of 'l' sounds, in the middle of each adjective and in the repetition of 'lands', interspersed with relatively lengthy vowel sounds ('-ough', '-ow', the 'a' in 'lands' drawn out in

the plural) inhibits swift or easeful reading. 'Hilly' breaks the general flow, the contrasting short vowel in the midst of patterning hinting at varying movement (up and down the hills?) or twists and turns in the journey. The tongue-twister element forces effort in the reading, making us more conscious of its deliberate craft. At some level it evokes and manifests the toil of Aengus's trek. Without the music of instrumental accompaniment, then, the poem retains its own patterning and play of sound. It is this aspect that is the focus of the next teaching stage: the features of the text that lead us to recognize this as a poem as well as a song.

The activity has so far focused on audio texts, so this is the time to introduce printed copies of the poem. This is partly a matter of balance. A listening activity directs attention to the aural characteristics of texts as well as fostering engagement. What I now want to do, conversely, is foster an appreciation of qualities that are inherent in the text. What resides in the words that is inherently poetic, in the dimensions other than those that overlap with song? What, ultimately, allows us to say 'The Song of Wandering Aengus' is a songpoem – a poem as well as the form its title declares for us? One strategy is to present to students the full printed text. The hollow lands/hilly lands example discussed showed an approach to considering and articulating the play of sounds conveyed even in print. A logical follow-up is to ask students to find a similar instance in stanzas one or two. I might also invite them to investigate what the song versions foreground through the singer's stress on specific nouns and adjectives.

Stage six: distinctions between poetry and song

The stages outlined should not be treated as a strict rule. I describe steps in a teaching sequence in order to articulate a rationale and indicate the interrelatedness of stages. Any stage can be amended, and sometimes they overlap. Stage six may not always be appropriate or even possible, as it depends on finding a further text that can provide new insight into the study poem for focus, and illuminates understanding of the differences between poetry and song. For this case study, good fortune led me to the song 'The Big Rock Candy Mountains' while also thinking about 'The Song of Wandering Aengus'. It begins like this:

> One evening as the sun went down
> And the jungle fires were burning,
> Down the track came a hobo hiking,
> And he said, 'Boys, I'm not turning
> I'm headed for a land that's far away
> Besides the crystal fountains

So come with me, we'll go and see
The Big Rock Candy Mountains.

(Harry McClintock, 1928)

The content the song shares with 'The Song of Wandering Aengus' is a serendipitous gift for the teacher. This is down to exactly matched lexis (*fire*, *went*, *land*) but also to direct narrative parallels. Both are accounts provided in a first-person voice by male travellers (evident in content or vocal performance), and both describe meetings with mysterious characters (the hobo, the girl). For each protagonist these provoke yearning for some magical or unattainable state of being. Both of these characters preserve mystery through anonymity: neither is named. The girl leads Aengus to imagine a mythical idyll that is otherworldly, yielding access to the fruits of the sun and the moon. The hobo points to a distant territory, the artifice of which is apparent in its name (*candy*) and the improbability of its detail (*crystal fountains*), which is further elaborated in its second verse:

In the Big Rock Candy Mountains,
There's a land that's fair and bright,
Where the handouts grow on bushes
And you sleep out every night.
Where the boxcars all are empty
And the sun shines every day
And the birds and the bees
And the cigarette trees
The lemonade springs
Where the bluebird sings
In the Big Rock Candy Mountains.

That the song originates in dustbowl America is relevant: it describes a utopia that would certainly have seemed unattainable at the time. Common to Yeats's poem is the evocation of a pastoral scene, similarly of trees, water, and sunshine. This parallel allows direct comparison of the presentation of environment in each text, with students evaluating the extent to which they find each presentation poetic.

The lyrics of 'The Big Rock Candy Mountains' show verbal patterning and organization of sounds. It comprises numerous full end-rhymes (*fountains/mountains*; *bees/trees*; *springs/sings*) and lines with internal coherence through assonance. The lines

There's a land that's fair and bright,
Where the handouts grow on bushes

contain unifying clusters of vowel sounds (three short *a*'s in the first; longer *o*/*u* sounds in the second) and crisper *t* sounds that pull both together. There is also a repeated formula where concrete nouns take on an adjectival function to produce 'jungle fires', 'crystal fountains', 'lemonade springs', and 'cigarette trees'. Consequently it is possible to discuss the song in terms familiar to students as the jargon of literary analysis: they can spot sound-features and identify phrases that create clear images in the mind.

'The Song of Wandering Aengus' begins with a comparable formula ('the hazel wood') and then describes the environment with the lines

> And when white moths were on the wing,
> And moth-like stars were flickering out.

Likewise we find patterning of sound, this time the whispering *w* sounds of the first and both short *i* vowels and clipped consonants (*t* and *k*/*ck*) in the second. The two lines are tied by the repetition of *moth*. I'm looking at the extent to which the use of sound may be enactive, a resource to convey something of the delicate yet twitchy movements of moths upon the air, and the transient and shifting stellar lights. And beyond the binding function of the repeated morpheme 'moth', what of its shift from noun to compound adjective that functions as simile? Is it to suggest unity and totality, either of Aengus's experience (the external does become internal elsewhere with the 'fire in my head') or in the interconnected harmony of his twilight world?

Earlier I isolated the line 'through hollow lands and hilly lands' to suggest its enactment of Aengus's journey. In the same stanza we find the line Holland altered,

> And walk among long dappled grass.

This also conveys the nature of movement, which becomes more relaxed and leisurely. The sedate mode of walking is communicated in the iambic metre and the regularity of internal vowel rhymes ('And walk'; 'among long'; 'dappled grass') that appropriately operate in pairs to describe the imagined couple. Certainly it creates a very different feel from the twisty disjunction implied at the stanza's opening.

In support of my teaching I thus arrive at the opinion that of these immediate texts 'The Song of Wandering Aengus' can be accorded status as a poem because sounds are used for something more than the patterning which the other text also exhibits. In Yeats's poem, the music of words is a resource for meaning. It is deployed to evoke something as intangible as mood, and plays on our feelings. Yeats anticipated that the poem would be encountered on the printed page, so for him this work was essential. The resource of musical accompaniment was not available unless in live performance. There is only language, and Yeats's poem provides its own meaningful music to an extent that 'The Big Rock Candy Mountains' does not.

Translating this hypothesis to classroom activity is not complicated. To promote evaluative thought, ask students: *To what extent do the words in each song create a mood?* Equally, it might be apt to suggest the concept of 'word music' and ask students to explore how it works in each text, according to these categories:

- patterning through repetition;
- patterning through end-rhyme;
- patterning through internal rhyme;
- patterning with sound for its own sake;
- patterning to suggest connections between words or items;
- patterning to echo or complement stated meanings or descriptions;
- patterning for which it is possible to suggest meaning, which may be different or even counter to stated meanings or descriptions.

The categories are not definitive. What matters is to give students the means to articulate the differing functions of sound patterning and reflect on its relationship with other ways of making meaning in a poem or lyric, especially lexical and syntactic. A more didactic approach would be to select lines rather as I did for discussion above, modelling the analysis and inviting students to apply the same to lines of their own choosing.

Resources
Recorded versions of 'The Song of Wandering Aengus' can be found on these releases:

Donovan, *HMS Donovan*, Beat Goes On Records, 2008 (original release 1970).
Jolie Holland, *Catalpa*, Epitaph, 2003.
Richie Havens, *Mixed Bag II*, Polydor, 1974.

Various live performances by David Gray can be found online, as can audio files of the above.

Other albums including Yeats's poetry performed as songs:

Carla Bruni, *No Promises*, Dramatico Entertainment, 2008.
The Speakers, *Yeats is Greats*, The Speakers, 2005.
The Waterboys, *Fisherman's Blues*, EMI, 1990 (includes 'The Stolen Child').

The Waterboys, *An Appointment with Mr Yeats*, Proper Records, 2011 (an entire collection).

Various Artists, *Now and in time to be*, Grapevine, 1997 (an entire collection).

The Yeats Society website has a full discography: http://yeatssociety.org

The work of other poets performed to music:

Emily Dickinson: Josephine Foster, *Graphic as a Star*, Fire, 2010.

Gerard Manley Hopkins: Sean O'Leary, *The Alchemist*, Earth Sweet Earth, 2005.

William Blake: Allan Ginsberg, *Songs of Innocence and Experience*, Klimt, 2012.

The website *The Muse's Muse* includes a forum discussing the differences between poetry and song:

http://www.musesmuse.com

Chapter 3

Poetry of place and nature: 'The Wild Swans at Coole'

Introduction

It is common for anthologies of poetry or sections within them to be organized according to their interest in place. Here I consider 'The Wild Swans at Coole' as a poem in which place is significant insofar as it influences decisions about how to approach the poem in the classroom. At the time of writing, the poem features in the anthology of the most widely taught examination specification in England and Wales, assigned to the thematic category of place, alongside other long-anthologized place poems such as 'Wind' by Ted Hughes and extracts of 'The Prelude' by Wordsworth. Through 'The Wild Swans at Coole' I draw out a way of thinking about and approaching poems considered to be poems of place that can be applied more generally.

The poem

'The Wild Swans at Coole' is the title poem for the collection in which it was published in 1919.

> **'The Wild Swans at Coole'**
> The trees are in their autumn beauty,
> The woodland paths are dry,
> Under the October twilight the water
> Mirrors a still sky;
> Upon the brimming water among the stones
> Are nine-and-fifty swans.
>
> The nineteenth autumn has come upon me
> Since I first made my count;
> I saw, before I had well finished,
> All suddenly mount
> And scatter wheeling in great broken rings
> Upon their clamorous wings.

I have looked upon those brilliant creatures,
And now my heart is sore.
All's changed since I, hearing at twilight,
The first time on this shore,
The bell-beat of their wings above my head,
Trod with a lighter tread.

Unwearied still, lover by lover,
They paddle in the cold
Companionable streams or climb the air;
Their hearts have not grown old;
Passion or conquest, wander where they will,
Attend upon them still.

But now they drift on the still water,
Mysterious, beautiful;
Among what rushes will they build,
By what lake's edge or pool
Delight men's eyes when I awake some day
To find they have flown away?

Like Yeats's poem, many of the anthologized poems describe real places. Coole Park is the ancestral home of the Gregory family, who were friends of Yeats, and the estate is now open to the general public, as described by Lady Gregory's granddaughter (Smythe, 1995: 6). After teaching 'The Wild Swans at Coole' as one of an anthology of Yeats's poems, I went to Ireland one summer and visited the park. You can now visit it online. It has its own tourist-oriented website where you will find a gallery of photographs, including one of the tree where Lady Gregory's acquaintances carved their autographs. The opportunity to sustain the association with swans has not been overlooked in the images.

It might seem a simple pedagogical judgement when teaching a poem of place to show students a photograph of the location evoked, perhaps even before they encounter the poem, but what might be the effect? Might it compromise the endeavour of studying the poem by shaping perception of the place too fully, or by limiting it to the perspective of a single gaze?

A photograph is possibly the most direct means of showing students the place as it is. In the high-definition projection it becomes visibly real, it exists. A poem about a real place likewise has a relationship with it, but what exactly? What might showing a photo first pre-empt or dictate?

'The Wild Swans at Coole' does more than describe a place. Given the title, it is clearly as much about the swans, yet, from the perspective of the poem's voice, it is also about a human experience. These three elements – a place, an item within that place, and the voice of the poem – are relevant to many poems. They constitute three tiers for consideration and decision-making in shaping a teaching approach.

Poems of place

The poet Edward Dorn, a specialist in the poetry of place, contends that poems create new places. Yes, a place exists as a real, physical, and material location, but these places do not exist with the qualities with which we as humans (or poets) might imbue them. Dorn sees the treatment of place in literature as active: 'you have to have a man bring it to you' (Dorn, 1961: 364). What he is concerned with is the experience of place, the matter of being in a place. Any poem ostensibly about place is actually an expression of being in, or relative to, a place. Within the poem, it must also follow that the place, though it exists elsewhere in material fact, is only real in the poem insofar as the poet constructs it. Dorn elaborates: 'place is brought forward fully in form, conceived entirely by it', the expression of place in the poem also constituting the 'activation of a man who is under its spell'. Because the place is integral to the poem, of the poem, it is 'not even extractable', and as far as the poem is concerned, 'it is then the only real thing'.

For 'The Wild Swans at Coole' the logic of this entails that it is a poem that makes a real Coole of its own. There is in Sligo, Ireland a material Coole Park, but this is something different from the Coole Park of Yeats's poem. The Coole of the poem is real on its own terms, as an expression of an experience of place. Any poem 'about' an actual place is not really so. Instead, the poem creates and constructs a new verbalized experience of that place. From the point of view of teaching and pedagogical judgement, this suggests that what we need to get at first with students is not in fact the place, but the voice, and hence the being that articulates their experience of place to us.

If we extrapolate from these considerations guidance to approaching poems concerned with nature or place, we might ask the following questions:

What do you know of the voice or persona describing this place?
How do you know about this voice? What information is provided?
What are they doing?
How do they feel?
What are they thinking?

Are their thoughts shaped by what they can see from where they are?
Or are they triggered by where they are: are they not really about the
details they see at all?
Or are they immersed in thoughts that seem to have no obvious
connection with where they are?

The last question will reveal the character of the poem, of any place poem. If some aspect of the place is articulated, it will be presented adjacent to other thoughts, though the fact of the juxtaposition will cause us to suppose some relationship between the two.

If our judgement is that the experience of place is the core concern of place poems, we might come at it another way. With students in mind, this is a more concrete approach which superficially concerns place rather than voice as the primary focus. If we ask students 'How would you feel in this place?', their thoughts are directed in at least one of three ways. First, they must at some level absorb and respond to information conveyed about the place of the poem. In turn, engagement with this information may necessitate activating their knowledge, whether intellectual or affective, of similar places (and this includes knowledge of representations of similar places, for instance if seen on film or encountered in other written texts). By implication, this concerns their being – existing – relative to such places or representations of places.

Finally, the students have to articulate how they would feel in this place and to synthesize and hypothesize with reference to this information. They might also distinguish how they would feel, in their own vocabulary, as distinct from the voice of the poem. To build from this foundation we can sustain attention to voice and feeling, overtly asking about the voice of the poem. Another option is to bridge this apparently broad and relatively open question with a question that requires students to articulate the triggers for the thoughts and feelings they have had so far, such as:

Which lines or words in the poem helped you imagine the place best?
Where in the poem can you find information that influenced how you
might feel in such a place?

The shift from word or line to less precisely defined information in these questions is significant too. The second question allows students to draw on aspects beyond those stated overtly and verbally, to elements of sound, symbol or form. It affords attention to aspects that may have affective power and act on readers or listeners, but which may be less easily contained in isolated quotation.

By way of demonstration, let us now try to apply these questions to 'The Wild Swans at Coole'. To which lines would we go first if we were first reading them for literal and immediately transparent information? The first stanza is full of literal detail:

> The trees are in their autumn beauty,
> The woodland paths are dry,
> Under the October twilight the water
> Mirrors a still sky;
> Upon the brimming water among the stones
> Are nine-and-fifty swans.

It is easy to see how students might refer to the images generated, given the panoramic and filmic presentation of the scene. Students could go further and draw detail from every stanza, but there is one valuable qualification which might have arisen from earlier attention to the voice: some of this location is experienced in the present, but much of it is recalled. If stanza one is of the immediate moment, what else is? Stanzas four and five are too, but not those stanzas in between. The first question might well direct students to those stanzas that are more immediate in their use of tense. Some responses to question two might recognize the difference and begin to explore the varying effect. This question may also elicit some engagement with the general mood, possibly described as pensive, still or meditative. In the first stanza the sheer economy of the line 'Mirrors a still sky' makes it stand out. It conveys a starkness of perception carried in its patterning of vowels and s sounds, in its contrast in length with the lines either side, and in the glassy perfection of the image.

An ecocritical orientation

An alternative approach less occupied with human experience and perception is to assume an ecocritical orientation to the text. Sasha Matthewman describes the approach in this way:

> First and foremost the teacher needs to engage deeply with the nature of the poem and the nature of the represented experience. This engagement with text and world is at the heart of an ecocritical approach and would be likely to involve investigation of the following related aspects: the representation of nature in the poem, including research into the natural and environmental context; the experience of nature that is described and how this

might relate to the students' experience; and the writer's experience and relationship to the natural world.

(Matthewman, 2011: 50)

Matthewman models an ecocritical approach to poetry through attention to the work of another Irish poet, Seamus Heaney, and his widely taught poem 'Death of a Naturalist'. She describes a sequence where pupils are presented with an image prior to reading the poem, here a photo of a flax-dam. The choice is stimulated by the poem's opening line,

> The flax-dam festered in the heart of the townland.

This judgement makes clear one significant emphasis of an ecocritical approach: to assimilate to the analysis of literature an engagement with the natural world it describes, if not firsthand then at least through research. In this case, an understanding of 'flax-dam' is considered essential to an appreciation of the poem, and thus the sharing of the picture acts as a reading cue, supporting comprehension when the term is encountered in the study text. With regard to theories of learning, this provides a relatively concrete prop for students, offering an iconic representation through visual stimulus (Bruner, 1966: 11) that supports understanding beyond and certainly differently from the verbal abstraction of the term. This is further confirmed in two activity prompts that foster responses to the picture which emphasize imagined experience. Pupils can be asked to describe what they see in the picture and speculate about what they think is happening and, furthermore, to:

> *Imagine that you visit the flax-dam later on a hot day when the flax has been rotting for some time. Describe what you find there in only ten lines, using all your senses.*

Following these suggestions, Matthewman asks students to read the first ten lines of 'Death of a Naturalist', and identify details Heaney uses to evoke the scene. The process illustrates her assertion that 'part of the teacher's preparation would be to think of analogies and anecdotes that might help to connect the experience in the poem with the experience of children in the class' (Matthewman, 2011: 51).

I became interested in Matthewman's description of an ecocritical approach to this poem because there appeared to be a clear parallel with 'The Wild Swans at Coole'. While Heaney's poem makes 'the lifecycle of the common frog ... the subject of the poet's imaginative and emotional attention' (ibid: 51), Yeats's poem has a similar interest in the lifecycle of the swan. Yet Matthewman's examples make clear that ecocritical approaches avoid formulaic steps to the study of poetry and indicate that judgement in this mode is just as likely to be informed by the distinctive character of each text and the natural phenomena or creatures they represent.

Because 'The Wild Swans at Coole' is apparently transparent in its description of a natural scene it may not require prefiguring through the use of images, though a pedagogical choice would be influenced by the nature of the class working with the poem. For instance, there could be students with no first-hand experience of seeing swans group together on a lake. For this example, however, I assume that students have some experience of such events, and instead focus on the ecocritical interest in researching the natural phenomena described in a text. In consideration of a prose text, Matthewman describes the value of finding out about the mockingbirds and bluejays in *To Kill a Mockingbird*, drawing on non-fiction metatexts to elucidate different attitudes to each expressed by characters in the novel.

Let us adopt a corresponding researcher's attitude to Yeats's poem, but look first within the text. On the face of it, this poem is less figuratively dense and far less allusive than many of Yeats's poems. It is possible to isolate details which can be interpreted as factual, free from the colour of metaphor, and separated from the shading of adjectives and adverbs. I adopt this approach because, like Matthewman, I incline to concreteness, aiming to find footholds for students as they begin to scrutinize the poem. A direct prompt can be shaped to assist their analysis: *List the facts provided about swans in the poem*. Though the task is simple, it is likely to – and intended to – trigger reflection upon Yeats's representation of them. As we shall see, there will be examples where disentangling facts from local colour helps us recognize features of Yeats's representation of the swans.

Here, then, are my efforts to isolate some factual details in the poem. Next to each selected quotation I provide a gloss, an attempt to articulate the information provided as a fact:

Table 3.1

Item	Stanza	Quotation	Gloss
A	1	upon the brimming water among the stones/are nine-and-fifty swans	Swans are found on or by water. Swans can be found in large groups.
B	2	all suddenly mount	Swans can take flight quickly.
C	2	scatter wheeling in great broken rings	Swans may fly in expansive circles.

D	2	clamorous wings	Swans' beating wings make noise.
E	3	the bell-beat of their wings	The movement of a swan's wing traces a shape similar to the outline of a bell. Alternatively, this is about how the beat sounds: at least it makes us think of a ringing bell.
F	4	They paddle ... in streams or climb the air	They can walk in streams, and thus in shallow water. They can fly.
G	5	they drift on the still water	They can stay afloat on the surface of water without having to swim.
H	5	Among what rushes will they build / By what lake's edge or pool	They build something (probably nests) within rushes and by the bank/shore or water.
I	5	they have flown away	After grouping at a location they fly away (it seems together).

Consistent with an ecocritical approach, this activity immediately directs attention to the swans and their behaviour in this environment. Yet gathering this information is the start of subtle analysis, as it permits consideration of 'problem' cases that begin to suggest something of Yeats's choices as a writer. The record of the collective items also tells us something about distribution of attention in the poem, showing the points at which the persona of the poem is attentive to the external fact of the swans as opposed to being engaged in his own ruminations upon them. The table shows that direct, naturalistic description of the swans is most frequent in stanzas two and five, with the other stanzas carrying less. The first stanza is focused mostly on the immediate environment of the swans, describing the trees, woodland, and water. Stanza three declares the persona's emotional state ('now my heart is sore') and dwells on memories of 'the first time on this shore', noting that 'all's changed'. Stanza five merits closer inspection: it does concern the swans, but few of its details can be viewed as factual.

The table can be used in a different way. In the process of identifying possibly factual details, one can't help noticing Yeats's use of modifiers and their effect. With reference to item A, we assume swans group together, but are left with the question around the number. Is it common that there are so many? If not, this is curiously specific. Why this precision, and why does Yeats invert the number? We also notice the adjective describing the water ('brimming') which is more suggestive of abundance than a more commonplace phrase like 'high tide'.

In stanza two, adverbs and adjectives begin to suggest something of the majestic, awesome qualities attributed to the swans: 'suddenly' applied to their launch (item B), 'great' to their rings of flight (C), and 'clamorous' to the noise of their wings (D) combine to colour more literal descriptions, and hint at movement on the edge of control, especially where the swans also 'scatter wheeling'. There is power here, contained, but only just. If a fact can be deduced from 'bell-beat' (E), the phrase is nevertheless a figurative compound formulation, its craftedness accentuated by virtue of alliteration. Similarly, the verbs of movement (F, climb; G, drift) hint at an impossible grace, the paradox that they both gain a foothold on the intangible, and move where all else is still.

Like 'bell-beat', and perhaps 'climb the air', there are numerous phrases not included in the table above that have a similarly figurative character, but which cannot be said to suggest the likely behaviour and capabilities of swans in reality. Once we have distinguished between the factual and the non-factual we can see the qualities which are attributed to these swans via the perception of the poem's persona. In 'those brilliant creatures' (stanza 3) the adjective is a subjective attribution, and it has an intensifying effect similar to that of a superlative. In stanza four, the veracity of detail is more complex, as the description takes on an anthropomorphic character: the swans are cast as creatures capable of love and pairing together ('lover by lover'); as perennially resistant to fatigue ('unwearied still'); even as ageless ('their hearts have not grown old'). Whether their togetherness makes the cold streams 'companionable' or if they are at one with the streams in nature is unclear, but these relationships are imagined and attributed.

Of particular interest from an ecocritical perspective is the stanza's concluding couplet:

Passion or conquest, wander where they will,
Attend upon them still.

Here the abstract nouns, and hence qualities that are categories of human thought, are said to 'attend upon' the swans. Once one is aware of the ecocritical interest in representation, this phrase with the intensifying conjunction 'upon' can be interpreted as representation revealed. It suggests the application of these concepts to the swans, but in recalling a relationship of servitude ('attend upon') could also be read as confirming the inferiority of this conceptual realm to the fact, the indisputable physical presence and being of the swans. A connected recognition is described in the poem as the swans escape the persona's view: 'when I awake some day / To find they have flown away'. In naturalistic description, in the reality of the world of the poem, they escape the persona's gaze. It seems he can no longer attribute qualities ('mysterious, beautiful') to the swans, but is left instead to speculate that others may do the same as the swans 'delight men's eyes' elsewhere. Yeats did not intend this poem to demonstrate an ecocritical stance, but he does subtly draw attention to its representative work by suggesting the thoughts of the persona as he contemplates the swans.

Not all poems have this reflexive attitude, but we can generalize the steps taken here so they can inform teaching decisions around other poems of place and nature. Framed as questions, guiding considerations can be expressed thus:

> *Is an ecocritical perspective relevant to the poem in terms of its content?*
>
> *What form of research is pertinent in order to have an informed understanding of the location, phenomena, or creature described? Is there detail in the poem that can begin the research process?*
>
> *How is the representation of nature mediated in the poem? Is it consistently conveyed as given, or does it at any point become self-aware?*
>
> *What can be gained from the study of the poem in terms of developing an understanding of the creature or environment described?*
>
> *What does the poem reveal or elucidate of the relationship between humans and nature?*

Conclusion

My approach with 'The Wild Swans at Coole' has taken 'the significance of the animal into account for its own sake' (Matthewman, 2011: 67) though the poem has simultaneously enhanced our understanding of the human experience. Yeats has deployed this representation of the swans with a tendency to anthropomorphism, that is 'the attribution of human feelings or traits to non-human beings or objects of natural phenomena' (Buell, 2005: 134). Matthewman identifies seven categories of anthropomorphic representation, and it seems 'The Wild Swans at Coole' is predominantly one of 'naturalistic description – animals are described in a real environment'. The definition allows for the possibility that human feelings may be ascribed to the animals, as they clearly are, and increasingly so, as the poem unfolds.

It is through this development that we can infer something of the persona's feelings. Though there are 'nine-and-fifty swans' we are given no information to suggest he is accompanied by any human. The persona is at once interested in the swans to the extent that he counts them, as he evidently did previously: 'The nineteenth autumn has come upon me / Since I first made my count'. Somewhat reflexively, the persona also counts the years, though it is clear this act of enumerating the passing time does not reverse the power of nature: syntactically, the 'me' of the poem is the object of autumn's verb, and thus nature as time has its effect on him where it does not, as he perceives it, upon the swans. The shift in time, marked by the parallel events of then and now, points up contrasting feelings on each occasion: 'now my heart is sore' where previously the persona 'trod with a lighter tread'. By implication his tread is heavy, not 'unwearied' like the swans. In writing 'their hearts have not grown old' Yeats has made a decision to use the negative, not a positively phrased assertion such as 'their hearts are forever young'. By using 'not grown old' he posits the possibility that the persona's heart, by contrast, has. While passion or conquest 'attend ... still' upon the swans, it seems they have in time taken hold of the persona and had their effects, for good or ill. The final stanza presses home the persona's solitary existence. Three times the swans are collectively referred to as 'they', consolidating our sense of their group. By contrast, the persona concludes the poem bereft even of their company, awaking 'some day / To find they have flown away'. He himself has not known a collective existence such as theirs and seems instead inclined, perhaps like all humans, to reverie or contemplation, the self-consciousness that permits the knowledge of the 'sore heart'.

The apparently naturalistic description of the location offered in the opening stanza corroborates this feeling. Not only does the expression of experience we receive as the poem originate in a setting that provides a natural mirror ('Under the October twilight the water / Mirrors a still sky'), it seems also that the scene is set apart. The sequence of the poem first describes trees, then 'woodland paths', then the 'October twilight', then the water mirroring the sky. It is as if we and the persona journey through the woods, through darkness, to the half-light of the mirror. In this scene, too, the persona arrives at a form of self-knowledge. Recalling Dorn, 'place is brought forward fully in form' as a consequence of this sequential presentation, such that the reader's experience of place mirrors that of the poem's persona. The sequence enacted in the poem encourages the reader's empathy with the persona's perspective, insofar as their experience of activity on the lake coincides. This is akin to what Jonathan Bate (2000) identifies as the poet's ability to bring the world into presence, to give us the sense or trace of the experience of another being in the world. In this poem, Yeats makes us deeply aware of the gulf between our lived experience and that of the swans. The pedagogical approach, informed by ecocriticism, draws out the artifice and craft required to mark the distance that might otherwise be only partially perceived by students, still less articulated.

Resources

Coole Park website: www.coolepark.ie

Chapter 4

Finding a centre: 'The Second Coming'

Introduction

Complex poetry tends to explore several ideas simultaneously, and it can defy sure explanation. Where classroom-based study and the demands placed on students to write about poems in examination settings entail paraphrasing, summarizing, and commentary, this is challenging precisely because poetry can convey meaning in ways that prose usually does not. It can, for example, draw on the resources of rhythm, form, and symbolism in crafted interworking that is more deliberate than might occur in conventional language. From a teaching perspective recognizing how hard it can be for students to find their bearings with a poem is a useful starting point, especially when the poem deals with difficult ideas or unfamiliar reference points, or if it is oblique in character. The teacher's role is to help students find a way into it, to get a foothold that supports orientation so they can begin to reach an understanding of what it can convey and how it does so. Given that poems are many and diverse, what thought processes might a teacher work through to select a route into the poem? Because the possibilities of approach are many, how do they consider the options and make judgements about their choice of path?

The poem I use as the basis for this exploration is Yeats's 'The Second Coming'. If you are unfamiliar with this poem this could be to your advantage here, because when you first read it you are likely to empathize with a student who is dealing with a challenging text for the first time. It is probably a poem for study with post-16 classes; my own initial encounter with it was in my first semester at university. I remember it vividly: the tutor presented a group of six or seven of us with the poem at the start of the seminar, then left the room for some minutes while we considered it. We knew through the established conventions of these sessions that he would select one of us to initiate discussion, and I recall the sound of his footsteps in the corridor, just before he came back in. I must have had an acute sense of my own discomfort with the poem, a feeling that I would be unable to comment with any confidence in my assertions because I found it so difficult and so unlike anything I had seen previously. This feeling of dread is not uncommon for students as they anticipate being chosen to present their provisional thoughts before their peers. In this moment, and even though dread is an emotion quite in tune with the mood of 'The Second Coming', I was less than delighted that the tutor's first words once he took his seat were 'John, can you start us off please?'

The poem
The poem was published in the 1921 collection *Michael Robartes and the Dancer*.

> **'The Second Coming'**
> Turning and turning in the widening gyre
> The falcon cannot hear the falconer;
> Things fall apart; the centre cannot hold;
> Mere anarchy is loosed upon the world,
> The blood-dimmed tide is loosed, and everywhere
> The ceremony of innocence is drowned;
> The best lack all conviction, while the worst
> Are full of passionate intensity.
>
> Surely some revelation is at hand;
> Surely the Second Coming is at hand.
> The Second Coming! Hardly are those words out
> When a vast image out of *Spiritus Mundi*
> Troubles my sight: somewhere in the sands of the desert
> A shape with lion body and the head of a man,
> A gaze blank and pitiless as the sun,
> Is moving its slow thighs, while all about it
> Reel shadows of the indignant desert birds.
> The darkness drops again; but now I know
> That twenty centuries of stony sleep
> Were vexed to nightmare by a rocking cradle,
> And what rough beast, its hour come round at last,
> Slouches towards Bethlehem to be born?

Preparing an approach: towards scaffolded reading
Being self-conscious about your own reading pathways can help you identify ways of approaching a text that are tailored to its unique character and demands. This assists in maintaining empathy with students' experiences of reading, and thus helps you articulate what can happen when someone reads

a poem, whether in the mind, cognitively, or taking account of the influence on the emotions, the affective dimension. This foundation informs how you shape a staged process that helps students into the poem.

The structuring of learning processes has been termed 'scaffolding', derived from the work of Jerome Bruner (1966). Robert Gagné (1970: 285) extends this thinking by articulating it at work in the structure of a lesson as 'instructional events'. He described learning across the unit of a lesson falling in eight events, each with a distinct purpose. These, in sequence and paraphrased, are to:

1. activate the learner's motivation;

2. inform the learner of the learning objectives;

3. direct the attention of the learner;

4. stimulate the learner to recall their relevant prior learning;

5. provide the learner with guidance for their learning activity whether a process, exercise, or activity;

6. enhance the capacity of the learner to retain the knowledge, skills, or understanding developed in the fifth event;

7. promote the learner's ability to transfer what has been learnt to other situations and contexts;

8. elicit the performance of the learner in the process, exercise, or activity and provide the learner with feedback about their performance.

The present discussion is most concerned with steps five to eight: sharing with students the poem, helping their engagement and comprehension, consolidating their learning, and shaping activities that develop their understanding and make it manifest to the teacher. Knud Illeris has noted Gagné's attention to the 'intellectual or subject matter' for learning (Gagné, 1970: 25), asserting a divergence from a tendency in progressive education to show 'little interest' in subject matter content, preferring to emphasize 'human development as a whole' (Illeris, 2007: 76).

Certainly 'The Second Coming' demands that particular details are addressed, and the different allusions, from the Second Coming itself to the gyre image, are presented in unique juxtaposition. The stimulus material needs distinctive treatment. Making connections between your knowledge of how students might read the text at hand and the principles of scaffolding helps shape attention to the poem that is sufficiently specific to do justice to its subtleties, while ensuring the design of the experience aids students in their learning.

First, the reading process: experienced readers know that it is possible to get a foothold on the text even if they cannot conquer it entirely. This means they continue in their reading even if there are details they cannot deal with immediately. When first reading from the page, these readers are likely to check their own comprehension, to self-monitor. When I read 'The Second Coming' for the first time, the opening line immediately presented a challenge. I had no familiarity with the word 'gyre' and had the associated difficulty of decoding the word: should it be vocalized with a hard or a soft *g*? Clearly for me as a teacher this signals something to address, though the significance of the item for readers is at this stage unclear. I felt able to comprehend most of the first stanza insofar as the rest of the vocabulary was familiar to me, though the way in which certain words worked together caused me problems, as some collocations appeared to jar. How can 'anarchy' be 'mere anarchy'? What exactly is the 'ceremony of innocence'? And though I could appreciate the general idea that 'the best lack all conviction' I was puzzled by 'the worst / Are full of passionate intensity' and the possibility that 'passionate intensity' could be perceived so negatively. Here is a generalizable principle of identifying before teaching the phrases that lack immediate transparency. These may not always pose a challenge through obscure reference or figurative play of language. As with the examples provided, it may be that the vocabulary of these phrases seems accessible but in their immediate context they present a challenge.

The poem was also challenging according to what I did or did not bring in terms of my own knowledge. This frames reading in terms of prior knowledge and as an associative web (see Meek *et al.*, 1977), where reading is a process calling on both textual and metatextual detail. I was familiar with the concept of the Second Coming and its religious significance, and could therefore establish a network of meaning across the second stanza between this repeated item and both 'a rocking cradle' and 'Bethlehem', though for me the very fact of this religious lexis was intimidating. I was not confident in my knowledge and understanding of biblical detail, so was aware that some allusions in the poem could be lost to me. The phrase *Spiritus Mundi* immediately confused and intimidated, both because it derived from Latin and because it suggested a spiritual discourse unknown to me. I was more secure with the imagery of the sphinx-like creature but unsure of its relationship to the Christian belief in the Second Coming. At least the sequence of the poem helped me understand that here it was related to the *Spiritus Mundi*, which could itself be construed as some form of collection or archive.

These various and slight difficulties do not quite convey the challenge of comprehending the poem satisfactorily. For though the details inhibiting a surface understanding are few, they affect my ability to put the poem together, to construct meaning from its images. The three layers of reading identified by Peter Guppy and Margaret Hughes (1999) are apposite. The first constitutes 'reading the lines': decoding and having an understanding of sentences at a literal level. A second requires 'reading between the lines', which encompasses identifying voice and position, or tolerating figurative meaning, or possibly several interpretations at once. The third layer is 'reading beyond the lines': drawing on knowledge and making links with information beyond the text. I might understand that this part of the poem describes a cataclysmic lurch to anarchy, and understand that a sphinx-like creature lurches to Bethlehem, but this doesn't get me any closer to appreciating why Yeats links these things or what import the fantastic creature of the sphinx might have relative to events in the material world beyond the poem. At some point in teaching, then, it might be appropriate to introduce metatexts that support interpretive work, but I choose not to do this immediately. First, I want students to make their own connections across the poem, but to give them some gentle support.

How do I do this with a poem? First, I set about identifying a number of broad ideas or images that I believe are important to making sense, and this is where the teacher's experience as a reader – both informal and perhaps by qualification in literary studies – becomes important. The items I choose are unlikely to be exhaustive: where an established body of critical work on a text exists, my selections might not match the breadth of interpretation found there. Just as important as received opinion is my knowledge of my students, especially my sense of what they find engaging and their collective ability to work with chosen material. For me this often links with avoiding clutter, and not offering too much supplementary detail. As much as possible, I want them to glean things from the text with their own impetus.

After my first experience of encountering the poem shared above, I worked through steps to find the meaning of 'gyre'. One way to do so is to follow connections in a way that is consistent with the concept of collocation, seeking words that the logic of the poem suggests will go together. I understand that gyre is a noun and that it is special in character ('widening'), and I might also be sensitive to its association with circular movement ('turning and turning') around a fixed point (though the 'centre cannot hold'). I might also surmise it is associated with falconry within the poem, and this might conjure for me the circling motion of a bird of prey. The reader might know the word 'gyrate', which affirms this notion of a circular motion. If I consulted a dictionary it would corroborate these speculations, offering spiral motion, cycle, or revolution. Even if I were unfamiliar with Yeats's special use of the term (and I might well be), the last of these definitions, if not each of them, could resonate with the rest of the poem. I might recognize several descriptions of significant and violent change ('things fall apart', 'anarchy is loosed', 'the Second Coming is at hand') that might be viewed as revolutions in the historical sense. So, by tracing links across the poem, it is possible to arrive at a speculative view that the poem is concerned with revolutions in time, and possibly that the word gyre is introduced to capture this.

When I took responsibility for teaching the poetry of Yeats to an A-level class, I did whatever any teacher of literature might and engaged in some research, trawling a collection of critical works about Yeats and scanning indexes for 'The Second Coming' or gyre. The internet makes such research far easier. It doesn't take long to find an explanation of Yeats's interest in alternative spiritual systems and the importance of the 'gyre' to his conception of history. Knowing the context of a work supports the teacher. Recognizing the importance of this initially arcane term informs a key judgement for learning around this poem: that it is necessary that students have a secure understanding of gyre and can engage with it on literal and symbolic levels. If so, they are likely to be far more satisfied in their reading of the poem. Another key judgement follows: that if this concept of the 'gyre' is so pivotal, it is essential that I support all students in articulating concisely what it is and, further, that I equip students with the skills to assimilate and then synthesize their understanding so they can make reference to it flexibly, for example, when making links between this idea and other lines in the poem. And this provides a thread that if followed will occupy a fair amount of teaching time. If this becomes the unifying thread for teaching around the poem, how do I draw attention to the breadth of the poem, to do justice to it in its entirety?

Next, I consider how the gyre can be linked to other key ideas in the poem, and again use detail in the poem to cue my process of selection. Because it gives the poem its title and because it is repeated, I am drawn to see the Second Coming as requiring discrete attention. Because of its unfamiliarity I must also deal with *Spiritus Mundi*. And I am compelled to reflect upon the journey of the sphinx because it dominates the second half of the poem.

Shaping a shared experience of the poem

The teacher of poetry in the classroom must find a way to support the reading process for individuals through the public and collective event of the lesson. The teacher's knowledge of how students could orientate to the poem will shape the lesson. The above discussion indicates that the following stages are necessary. They are presented in a generalized statement and with an illustration of what this means for 'The Second Coming'.

The sequence of teaching: items for consideration

Table 4.1

General item	Details for 'The Second Coming'
Initial reading of the poem	Selecting the mode of encounter most appropriate to this poem. Possibly hearing it first to capture the sense of uncertainty and fear, then reading from the page.
Dealing with unfamiliar vocabulary: vocalization, definition, understanding	Gyre and *Spiritus Mundi* both need some attention. As a central idea, *anarchy* needs to be clear.
Dealing with lexis that comes from a specialist discourse	This poem includes vocabulary associated with Christian beliefs: the Second Coming; revelation; Bethlehem. The 'ceremony of innocence' and the 'rocking cradle' may also be connected.
Dealing with related items/allusions	Both the sphinx and the falcon merit consideration. There is a potential link, in that the falcon represented two Egyptian deities.
Outlining the narrative of the poem	A movement is traced from stanza one in which 'things fall apart'; through two where there is a call for revelation, and the sphinx begins its movement, to where there is finally a new birth in darkness.
Identifying core concepts/images	The gyre refers to circular movement echoed in reel but also in the historical cycle described in the poem.
Space to explore/articulate/paraphrase	Allow students time to engage with each element described above, and to articulate them in their own words.
Not necessarily providing meaning – but giving students space to construct meaning	Select resources that clarify the allusions and indicate the historical context for the poem.

Students writing about the poem	Students will need the skills to articulate the distinctive elements of the poem. They will need to rehearse writing that is similarly distinctive to this study. For example, they need to use sentence structures and vocabulary that adequately describe gyres and their relevance to the text.

If I want to guide students' thinking towards the key ideas, I can do it in a way that offers them some autonomy. Once beyond the initial reading, I can direct them towards these by asking them to locate phrases according to a specific prompt, but allow them choice over which prompt to take up. For instance:

a) *To prefigure shared attention to the concept of gyres*

Identify words or phrases in the poem that you associate with circling movements. You may wish to distinguish between those you know are directly relevant and those which you speculate are connected.

b) *To direct students' attention to the sphinx and to trace the short narrative of its movement*

A 'rough beast' is described in the penultimate line. List what you learn about it from the poem.

and

c) *To take account of students' possible knowledge of religious events*

If you recognize the notion of the Second Coming mentioned in lines 10 and 11, to what extent does the Second Coming described in the poem match your expectations? Make a note of details that either confirm or confound these.

The most open use of prompts like these allows students to begin with their preference, possibly in pairs, to encourage hypothesizing. Alternatively, the prompts could be explored in sequence. Each engages the students in gently scaffolded attention to discrete conceptual areas of the poem. Once students have responded to the prompts, the sequence of reporting on their ideas is likely to encourage links across the domains. Though no teacher can predict what connections students will make, presenting these areas for consideration concurrently creates a frame and is likely to develop thought around them far more quickly than without this sequencing. The principle of choice does allow for one or even two of the three not being selected. The teacher can use the students' selection as a form of diagnostic assessment. Where they choose one prompt over others, they probably perceive it as the priority, but also feel most comfortable with it. I would prepare my own responses in anticipation of the plenary discussion following these prompts, and then shape a second tier of questions to guide students still further around each prompt.

The teacher needs either to confirm the hypotheses of students or to introduce secondary information to support their consideration further. The supporting texts should be limited so that they can be assimilated relatively quickly. They should genuinely inform reading of the core text but not distract from it either by demanding too much time of the reader or providing detail that itself might need explanation. In the case of Yeats's conception of history, a single judiciously chosen extract of his own work or a biographical work might suffice. The teacher's judgement is important: to select from a range of sources and to abridge if this focuses the lesson on the core text.

My preferred strategy for presenting the secondary text to students is simple. The first stage is to offer the new text as a new prompt for discussion by setting it alongside the core text. What connections can students make between poem and secondary text? Have a route of further support prepared: for example, to wonder aloud:

> *If we take this statement here about the gyres – that they expand and diminish – are there lines in the poem which relate to its widest point?*
> *What does the poem suggest of these stages in the cycle?*
> *Can you suggest adjectives that describe these stages?*

Another technique is to step out of close reading to attend to the centrality of the gyre concept and the importance that all students should understand it. Because it concerns movement, I ask students to replicate the movement of two interrelated gyres. This has the effect of demystifying a potentially difficult and abstract concept, supporting understanding through kinaesthetic and thus more concrete experience. The movement echoes the formation of ring-a-ring-a-roses, so makes students laugh, helps them relax, and allows them to visualize the movement of the gyre in three dimensions. An inner circle of students gradually moves outward from a central cluster, while the second larger outer circle draws nearer together, so eventually the two groups cross and exchange places. After initial rehearsal of the movement, the groups can replicate the movement and thus appreciate its cyclical character. In summary of the activity, students describe the movement they had enacted and share their descriptions with their peers. These are also descriptions of the movement of the gyres, a concept they may need to articulate in an assignment or in examination conditions. Most importantly, the concept is consolidated for them as a verbal expression.

The second prompt I suggested draws attention to the imagined horrific apocalypse brought by the 'rough beast' to Bethlehem. It directs students to the narrative conclusion of the poem, marking it as a focus for their attention. The third question attempts to build on prior knowledge, but also anticipates some use of metatexts given the significance of the Second Coming and its pre-eminence, marked by the poem's title.

In the elements to accommodate in the teaching sequence (see Table 4.1), I indicated associated specialist lexis that would need planned attention. One approach would be to offer explanations from reference sources such as dictionaries or encyclopaedias. However, because these allusions obviously originate in biblical stories, a few direct quotations would be useful. Matthew 24 provides Christ's declaration of the event of the Second Coming, and in concise form. Revelations is less economical, so an extract conveying an apocalyptic mood akin to Yeats's poem best suits the purpose of contextualizing the study text. Both in my view are more powerful resources than explanations or simple definitions of vocabulary, as they demonstrate the narratives Yeats evokes, and can help students understand Yeats's view of history as cyclical narrative.

Attending to 'anarchy' and the poem's presentation of revolution, in the sense of both revolving motion and violent historical change, invites a similar approach. 'The Second Coming' was written in 1919 in the aftermath of the First World War. Earlier drafts made reference to revolutions across Europe, in France, Ireland, Germany, and Russia. There would be merit in sharing those, but using a short quotation would signal the correspondence of the poem to Yeats's own era. Also in 1919 and in an Ireland volatile after the Easter Rising, Yeats wrote to his friend George Russell, 'I consider the Marxian criterion of values as in this age the spearhead of materialism & leading to inevitable murder' (in Ellmann, 1961: 232, note 2). A similar attitude can be found in another of Yeats's poems, called 'The Statues': 'We Irish, born into that ancient sect / But thrown upon this filthy modern tide / And by its formless spawning fury wrecked'. Yeats's combined anguish and fascination with the state of Europe can also be linked to the rise of Modernism in art and culture, which presented 'a pluralized, complex and ununifiable universe' (Bradbury, 1971: 31). All of these trends are relevant to a poem that asserts 'the centre cannot hold'. However, the complexity of the poem is such that if the teacher uses metatexts, they should not divert attention from the detail of the poem itself. To orchestrate these different prompts in practical terms could mean presenting to the class whatever range of quotations the teacher considers necessary, inviting them to suggest connections between the main text and the related selections. Alternatively, different quotations could be allocated to different student groups, thus permitting the quotations to be distributed according to the capacity of each group to handle them. The Bradbury quotation, for instance, may be challenging due to its tangential relevance to the poem, whereas the phrase from 'The Statues' ('filthy modern tide') could be easier for students to work with as it directly echoes the 'blood-dimmed tide' of 'The Second Coming'.

The main aim of providing selected material beyond the study text is to elucidate its detail, to spotlight specific ideas or vocabulary, and to help students understand them more fully. I limit the additional material so as not to distract students' attention from the development of the linked ideas in the study text, for it is there that I want the weight of their interpretive work to be. So I would limit attention to *Spiritus Mundi* to a brief gloss: it is a universally shared consciousness or memory store or, in contemporary analogy, a worldwide web of the mind. Likewise, though the falcon has symbolic resonance in both Irish and Egyptian lore (in the latter as both the Sun God Ra and Horus), those references can be deferred or omitted so as to concentrate on the 'falcon cannot hear the falconer' as a metaphor that can yield helpful interpretation without extra-textual knowledge.

Conclusion

The approach outlined in this chapter demonstrates the sorts of judgements needed to develop a coherent approach to texts that make many allusions. It is easy to get distracted by allusions and forget to attend to the detail of the study text before you. The judgements concern which details should be emphasized and to what degree: deciding which allusions may not require full explanation, either because their relevance may appear slight to students until they have engaged with the poem more fully, or because they might introduce distracting tangents that reduce attention to the prominent items in the text. It may be that after identifying elements for clarification (see Table 4.1), the teacher finds related reference sources supporting engagement and deeper understanding of the source texts. Nevertheless, the teacher's work is subject to available time and resources: the perfect metatext rarely comes to notice without a good deal of searching.

Ultimately, the search echoes the imagery of the poem for attention. The teacher's work is to hold a centre with some consistency for students; to keep in touch with the poem whatever the temptation to digress, just as Yeats wishes the falcon still to hear its falconer.

Chapter 5
Making parallels: 'Sailing to Byzantium' and getting there

Introduction

This chapter considers using two texts together, where doing so brings insights to the study of each. Presenting them together assumes they are somehow connected, perhaps by topic, common author, or shared form – the reasons vary. In some instances an exact pairing may be defined for teachers; for example, a textbook may set two texts side by side. Presenting poems in tandem, on the other hand, is a frequently used device in examinations.

Alternatively, the teacher may work with a small collection of poetry prescribed for them, as with an anthology compiled by an examination board. The anthology might be arranged along thematic lines (for example, poems of place, war, or love); according to their cultural provenance (for example, 'from different cultures', or drawn from a canonized 'English heritage' list); or according to era or literary movement. Though these classifications present boundaries, the teacher at least retains some agency in pairing or grouping poems drawn from them.

Finally, the teacher might be free, limited only by their imagination and professional judgement. They determine what might be of pedagogic value through a juxtaposition of poems. Whatever the option open to them, teachers will have some control over the presentation of the poems. This chapter sets related deliberations in the context of Jean Piaget's theory of learning. Piaget believed that intelligence seeks 'an all-embracing equilibrium': that we strive to find sense in things, seeking coherence with what we know already. Interestingly, he quotes a contemporary (though not associate) of Yeats, professor of philosophy Leon Brunschvicg, who asserted that intelligence 'wins battles' and is 'like poetry, in a continuous work of creation' (Piaget, 2001: 10). The teacher's work outlined here is to assist students in that process, to ease their route 'along ever more complex paths' to equilibrium (ibid.: 9).

Considering the parallels

The pairing used here is consistent with the second illustration. As I worked with the collection of Yeats's poems prescribed by the examination board, I retained discretion over how to present poems to students and in what sequence. In a group containing the poems 'Sailing to Byzantium' and 'Byzantium' I opted to approach them as connected texts. These are some of the questions that became relevant to my preparations:

> *What are the merits of considering the poems together, and what is best left to looking at each poem in isolation?*
> *How should the pair be presented? What framing will be necessary, and what prompts or signals will be used to suggest a connection?*
> *Will the poems first be presented in a sequence, the second inevitably considered in the shadow of the first? Or should they be presented together on the same page?*
> *What elements will I choose to emphasize?*
> *What strategies will I adopt to foreground these elements, and how will the chosen mode of presentation contribute?*

I also need to determine the interaction my students will have with the poems:

> *Do I want to guide students to find similarities, differences, or both?*
> *Are there particular skills I want students to develop that can be transferred to studying other texts in parallel?*
> *Do students have the verbal resources for articulating parallels, and can they do so by addressing details in both texts as well as general text-level features?*

All these questions are concordant with supporting students' comprehension of the poems and their affective engagement and response.

The poems

The poems for comparison were published some five years apart. 'Sailing to Byzantium' first appeared in the 1928 collection *The Tower*, though it was written in 1927. 'Byzantium', written in 1930, was not published until 1933 as part of *The Winding Stair and Other Poems*.

'Sailing to Byzantium'
I
That is no country for old men. The young
In one another's arms, birds in the trees
– Those dying generations – at their song,
The salmon-falls, the mackerel-crowded seas,

Fish, flesh, or fowl, commend all summer long
Whatever is begotten, born, and dies.
Caught in that sensual music all neglect
Monuments of unageing intellect.

II

An aged man is but a paltry thing,
A tattered coat upon a stick, unless
Soul clap its hands and sing, and louder sing
For every tatter in its mortal dress,
Nor is there singing school but studying
Monuments of its own magnificence;
And therefore I have sailed the seas and come
To the holy city of Byzantium.

III

O sages standing in God's holy fire
As in the gold mosaic of a wall,
Come from the holy fire, perne in a gyre,
And be the singing-masters of my soul.
Consume my heart away; sick with desire
And fastened to a dying animal
It knows not what it is; and gather me
Into the artifice of eternity.

IV

Once out of nature I shall never take
My bodily form from any natural thing,
But such a form as Grecian goldsmiths make
Of hammered gold and gold enamelling
To keep a drowsy Emperor awake;
Or set upon a golden bough to sing
To lords and ladies of Byzantium
Of what is past, or passing, or to come.

'Byzantium'

The unpurged images of day recede;
The Emperor's drunken soldiery are abed;
Night resonance recedes, night walkers' song
After great cathedral gong;
A starlit or a moonlit dome disdains

All that man is,
All mere complexities,
The fury and the mire of human veins.

Before me floats an image, man or shade,
Shade more than man, more image than a shade;
For Hades' bobbin bound in mummy-cloth
May unwind the winding path;
A mouth that has no moisture and no breath
Breathless mouths may summon;
I hail the superhuman;
I call it death-in-life and life-in-death.

Miracle, bird or golden handiwork,
More miracle than bird or handiwork,
Planted on the starlit golden bough,
Can like the cocks of Hades crow,
Or, by the moon embittered, scorn aloud
In glory of changeless metal
Common bird or petal
And all complexities of mire or blood.

At midnight on the Emperor's pavement flit
Flames that no faggot feeds, nor steel has lit,
Nor storm disturbs, flames begotten of flame,
Where blood-begotten spirits come
And all complexities of fury leave,
Dying into a dance,
An agony of trance,
An agony of flame that cannot singe a sleeve.

Astraddle on the dolphin's mire and blood,
Spirit after Spirit! The smithies break the flood,
The golden smithies of the Emperor!
Marbles of the dancing floor
Break bitter furies of complexity,
Those images that yet
Fresh images beget,
That dolphin-torn, that gong-tormented sea.

The specific pairing: tracing connections

Given the shared interest both poems have with ancient Byzantium, there is evident merit in considering Yeats's presentation of the city in each. The fact that 'Sailing to Byzantium' preceded the more simply named 'Byzantium' makes it relevant to consider the development in Yeats's treatment of the focus, and the broader development of his poetic art. Still, when we think about presenting these poems to students who are probably unfamiliar with them and the city they describe, encountering both simultaneously may be overwhelming. So my approach with these two poems would be to present them initially one at a time, in the order they were published.

'Sailing to Byzantium' seems to be the poem most likely to speak to students directly without commentary, and which they can make more of independently. I come to this judgement via Piaget's discussion of how we group ideas (2001: 41), and his proposal that our approach to any problem or task is influenced by our experience of similar concepts in the past. 'Sailing to Byzantium' is the more direct of the two poems, both in presentation of an initial scene that can be understood by readers, and in style. Its first line, 'That is no country for old men', is an overt statement with straightforward syntax, while the next two lines in particular outline a vivid tableau: 'The young / In one another's arms, birds in the trees / – Those dying generations – at their song'. The vocabulary and the actions described are simple and recognizable, though the parenthetic 'Those dying generations' seeds something more complex, prompts an exploration of mortality, and prefigures the rest of the stanza and the poem. Contrast this with the early lines of 'Sailing to Byzantium':

> The unpurged images of day recede;
> The Emperor's drunken soldiery are abed;
> Night resonance recedes, night walkers' song
> After great cathedral gong;

Here the vocabulary tends to the polysyllabic, with a number of noun phrases outside the common idiom. I anticipate that these ideas are less likely to be part of students' existing experience, and that the poem will probably feel difficult to them: it will not be easy for them to find equilibrium through the text. In their interesting juxtapositions, 'unpurged images', 'Emperor's drunken soldiery' and 'night resonance' do not have the universality of 'Byzantium' and so cannot be readily grouped with familiar combinations. If they function to create a mood more effectively, they strike a different tone, which can be attended to once the poems are considered together.

Towards sequencing

The distinctions drawn between the two poems in their first few lines are generally true of the entire texts. 'Sailing to Byzantium' tends towards a simpler lexis, more frequently monosyllabic. Its imagery is likewise more direct, supported by organization of ideas through its four stanzas: first, the pastoral scene; second, 'an aged man'; third, the 'sages standing in God's holy fire'; and finally, the voice of the poem moving 'out of nature' to take the form 'Grecian goldsmiths make', such as a mechanical bird. Each stanza has clarity of focus usually signposted in its opening line, though the fact that the last implies rather than states the form of the bird shows that this poem too has subtleties. Through formal organization the poem contributes to the possibility of its concepts being assimilated by students such that they find equilibrium early in the teaching sequence.

Because 'Sailing to Byzantium' develops in this neat, staged manner, it appears to be a good platform from which to prepare students and build their confidence for study of 'Byzantium'. For the teacher there is serendipity in the title: this is preparation for 'Byzantium', the journey there. 'Byzantium' too has a discipline of organization, shifting from a stanza of exposition in which 'a moonlit dome disdains / All that man is' to an encounter with a floating image, then to description in the third (and this time explicit) of 'Miracle, bird or golden handiwork'. The penultimate stanza describes, again like the first poem, a fire ('flames begotten of flame / Where blood-begotten spirits come') and the poem concludes with a fifth stanza, evoking the images of dolphins set in the mosaic floors of the city. The two poems clearly have close parallels, so understanding 'Sailing to Byzantium' first becomes a means to grasp ideas to prefigure their treatment in 'Byzantium'.

Sequencing comprehension

How do I direct my approach to both poems, with this notion of prefiguring in mind? I want the study of one poem to give me a basis to support students' understanding of the other, a principle consistent with Piaget's theory of structures of thought. The ability to approach 'Byzantium' will eventually succeed similar competence with the simpler poem, such that 'one brings about a more inclusive and stable equilibrium' (Piaget, 2001: 7). For Piaget intelligence is 'thus only a generic term to indicate the superior forms of organization or equilibrium of cognitive structurings'. Students will be prepared to deal with 'Byzantium' because their problem-solving interpretive activity can work to a solution 'attained simply by extending and completing the relationships already grasped' (ibid.: 42).

John Gordon

In preparing to teach poems, a teacher is likely to reflect on what the poems seem to be about. In 'Sailing to Byzantium', that parenthetic phrase I mentioned becomes crucial, pointing out that the young embracing one another are – though they appear oblivious to it – also 'those dying generations'. The phrase is a prominent and useful pedagogical trigger for the exploration of mortality across both poems. So I trace it in 'Sailing to Byzantium' first, and can find it manifest further in this stanza and beyond. Most immediate are the lines 'Fish, flesh, or fowl, commend all summer long / Whatever is begotten, born and dies'. Abundance and insouciance are presented concurrent with the cycle of life and death. In the second stanza, an aged man is 'but a paltry thing ... unless / Soul clap its hands and sing'. Though bodily mortality is a fact, the poem contends that a soul can live on, and celebrate, transcending mortality. In the third stanza, an invocation for sages to come from the holy fire leads to this man's soul being untethered from its 'dying animal' body, to be gathered 'into the artifice of eternity'. Finally, the soul takes a new form that is artifice, that is crafted: the form of a golden bird that sings 'Of what is past, or passing, or to come'. This concluding line echoes in its three-part structure a phrase in the first, 'Whatever is begotten, born and dies', yet presents the passage of time with greater optimism. A teaching question arises from this last juxtaposition: what permits this new perspective? More directly, how – according to the poem – is it possible to outpace mortality? This last stanza suggests it is through art, and clarifies the earlier phrase 'monuments of unageing intellect'. Monuments and art share similar transcendental potential. In sum, tracing the idea across stanzas like this equips me with a clear line for my teaching.

Teasing out a thread like this is more difficult in 'Byzantium', because the treatment of mortality in it is less readily reduced to a comparable line of progression. Students need time to trace and engage with the exploration of mortality in 'Sailing to Byzantium' first. It strikes me as a necessary step in the teaching sequence. What approaches can be used initially with the simpler poem, to give students some agency in exploring these threads? Here are some possibilities.

The teacher isolates phrases linked by a common theme

After directing collective attention to the first stanza and the paradox of 'those dying generations' in the midst of youthful joy, isolate phrases that trace the theme. Present the quotations selected in the previous paragraph, then ask students to suggest connections between them.

Students select phrases and suggest links between them
Build from the same initial attention to the opening lines, and ask students to trace one or two phrases in each stanza that they believe explore the same theme.

Students classify phrases around concepts given by the teacher
Allocate a number of students to focus on 'life', another group on 'death', and to seek phrases across the poem that they associate with each. The point of interest in shared discussion arises when their lists appear to overlap – the phrases that draw together both strands. Either by allocating to further groups the terms 'immortality' and 'mortality', or by asking these first groups to apply the terms to their existing list, it may be possible to support nuanced distinction between the terms and the subtleties of the poem. Do phrases associated with 'immortality' necessarily correspond with those of 'life'? The framework, though simple, can help students to make distinctions within the poem and be alert to the differences between concepts.

Use the poem's title as a trigger for an open line of questioning
Exploit the poem's title and posit a question around travel, for instance, 'The title describes a journey to Byzantium by boat. What other journeys are described in the poem?' This affords space for students to identify the journey from life to death, and even of the cycles traced rather than simple A to B trajectories.

The opening stanza of 'Byzantium' assumes the reader knows about the city of Byzantium and its emperor. 'Sailing to Byzantium' provides this information step by step, so looking at it first prepares readers for the second poem. It helps that the notion of 'monuments to unageing intellect' and the perpetuity of art have been approached and understood, as the concepts are integral to the first stanza of 'Byzantium'. Further, attributed to the monument of the city dome is the assertion of its superiority over mortal human life. This is emphatic in both the verb 'disdains', and in the scope of its disdain of 'all that man is, / All mere complexities, / The fury and the mire of human veins'.

A teacher might feel, however, that the first stanza is not the best place to begin. Some close attention to the second stanza might be worthwhile, the phrase 'death-in-life and life-in-death' conveniently echoing the themes broached in the former poem. The phrase fits a formula that is used across 'Byzantium': a phrase is presented and then inverted as if the two concepts were interchangeable. The rest of this stanza, rather like the first, assumes knowledge of Hades (in Greek mythology, king of the underworld and god of death and the dead), and confirms the poem as more allusive than 'Sailing to Byzantium'. Some readers will find this allusiveness part of the poem's difficulty. 'Byzantium' describes an evocation of a spiritual entity ('a mouth that has no moisture and no breath') from beyond the human world ('I hail the superhuman'). As an event it is likely to be curious to students, and the poem lacks the relatively familiar contextual and explanatory detail of holy figures, though it describes the same phenomenon. For this reason too, 'Sailing to Byzantium' helpfully prefigures the second poem's obscure action. The stanza's first couple of lines also work to a formula that suggests the interconnectedness of words and states of being: 'Before me floats an image, man or shade, / Shade more than man, more image than a shade'. As well as working through the syntax to make sense of it in isolation, students and teacher can recognize the play and inversion in the words that is employed elsewhere in the poem.

Where students were introduced to the golden bird by inference in 'Sailing to Byzantium', here it is presented definitively but in a manner that captures something more of the superiority of art, which lies in its capacity to transcend. The first two lines of stanza three, 'Miracle, bird or golden handiwork, / More miracle than bird or handiwork', make clear in the nouns that the bird has the qualities of each item, but make emphatic the 'miracle' dimension. Likewise, that the bird is 'star-lit' links it with the 'starlit' dome as a further monument which similarly scorns 'complexities of mire and blood'. The stanza begins to make clear a network of ideas, an interconnectedness that is a feature of style as well as content. There are partial echoes of phrases that have gone before, retaining the sense but showing variation in expression. They function a little like the gently changing phrases in the poetic form of the villanelle, and likewise convey internal coherence and the paradox of cyclical movement within the inevitably linear progression of a printed poem. In the study of these two poems that becomes important, since the theme of both is cycles of life and death set beside transcendence through art.

The central position of this stanza as third of five is worthy of note. If the poem has development of plot or action, this is an aside, not part of the encounter with an image/spirit amid the city's pavements. Its location suggests, however, that in terms of the poem's exploration it is its very heart. If I choose to begin my teaching of any poem anywhere other than the opening line, I imply to students that we will be reading in a different way from usual. We are less concerned with content and chronology than we were with the first poem. The decision helps to underline structural characteristics other than linear progression, and marks the difference relative to 'Sailing to Byzantium'.

Hindsight: articulating the rationale

I shall draw away from the detail of poems for a moment and return to discussion of a pedagogical rationale for the chosen approach to the texts, so that the principles may be generalized to other works. What have I done so far?

- I have recognized that the poems consider a common topic (Byzantium), and that they share themes (following from mortality, these are immortality, transcendence, and the perpetuity of art).
- It has been possible to recognize shared imagery and events across the poems (the golden bird, evocation of spirits).
- I have decided on a teaching sequence to present the poems to students in the order of their publication.
- I have identified one poem as the more accessible, without the need for extensive explanation or the addition of supporting text. This is another factor in the decision to use this first in the teaching sequence.
- The first poem has sufficient information to give students an understanding of the topic (Byzantium).
- I have decided that the sequence and organization of the first poem can be exploited in teaching for two purposes: to help students comprehend the development of ideas in this text, and to prefigure their treatment in the second.
- I have concluded that the second poem presents paralleling themes, images, and events, but does so in a more allusive manner than the first.
- I have noticed that the second poem has some features of form that differ from the first. Both have linear development outlining a journey (from mortality to transcendence), though the second has aspects that enact circularity and interconnectedness.
- I have decided that because the first poem supports learning to establish content (topic and theme), and because the second poem considers the same topic but with different presentation, the focus of teaching around the second can concentrate more on form. In teaching, this distinction can underline the difference in form between the two.

The discussion of the detail of each poem shows that form in the second is of interest due to its intricacy and its relevance to the poem's theme. Students can begin to reflect on form with greater concentration, and the focus can be exploited as means to reflect on the complex treatment of ideas in the poem. In summary, across study of the two poems there is a progression from attention to ideas in the first, to the interplay in the second of form and ideas. The second stage represents a more authentic pedagogy of poetry, as the poem is treated as more than a receptacle for ideas: its form is recognized as an essential resource for making meaning, and the pedagogy begins to draw attention to this in tandem with the poem's verbal resources.

A metalanguage for looking at form

I have already used vocabulary to describe form for which students may require deliberate and staged introduction. To discuss subtleties of form well they need the language: not just the names and conventions of forms, but also the resources to describe their effects.

To comment on the form of both poems, the students will find it useful to understand the following terms (examples in parentheses are drawn from each):

Table 5.1

Stanza	'Sailing ...' has four; Byzantium five
Rhyme scheme	'Sailing ...' *abababdd* and 'Byzantium' *aabbcddc*; both eight-line stanzas
Full-rhyme	thing/sing; disdains/veins
Half-rhyme	young/song; cloth/path
Couplets	in 'Sailing ...' they end each stanza; in 'Byzantium' they are internal

In addition, the words *narrative, sequence, progression, linear, linearity, cycle, circular, repetition,* and *echo* are pertinent, and you may nominate others. Students will also need terms to describe the role of form in communicating concepts connected with time and circularity, such as *manifests, realizes, makes concrete, enacts.*

No element of these lists is prescriptive. This cannot be a single approach – you decide your lists according to your chosen emphases for study and the characteristics of the poems. What is generalizable is identifying and then teaching the relevant metalanguage. And students need to be able to use sentence structures that support comparison or contrast, such as:

in both poems Yeats uses ...
each text demonstrates use of ...
the two poems show ...

and for contrast, phrases such as:

> *the first poem is unique in …*
> *the second alone uses …*
> *'Sailing' uses … while 'Byzantium …'*

These stems might seem obvious, but it is worth modelling their application to whichever poems are the immediate object of study so that students can see how to express the distinctions clearly.

Form and effect

One would hope to be able to promote versatile thinking about the poems' formal traits that can be applied to any number of texts. Recognizing the distinction between full- and half-rhymes is useful only insofar as students can identify each and comment on their significance in context. It may matter only if a rhyme is incomplete where it follows a sequence of full rhymes, or conversely a full rhyme may acquire salience only in the midst of a pattern of half-rhymes. The pedagogic aim is to make students sensitive to these variations, and able to judge whether they are significant according to their effect on the listener's or reader's inner ear. Students may also need guidance in classifying these effects, for instance, pairs draw together two ideas in rhyme, or enact some conflict or dissonance described in action or event through disruption of patterns in sound. The variation may sometimes be more innocuous, to suggest the rhythms of everyday speech and disguise the artifice of the poem's patterning.

It is interesting to speculate over the effect of an example like this, a trio of rhymes from 'Sailing to Byzantium' where two full-rhymes are followed by a half-rhyme, and a corresponding shift in rhythm:

> *birds in the trees*
> *mackerel-crowded seas*
> *begotten, born and dies*

or this from the third stanza of 'Byzantium' describing the golden bird:

> *… by the moon embittered, scorn aloud*
> *In glory of changeless metal*
> *Common bird or petal*
> *And all complexities of mire or blood.*

Why is there an imperfect rhyme here, to end a line describing mortal creatures? What is the relevance or resonance of the dissonant d consonants, close to the hard c sounds of 'scorn', 'common', and 'complexities'?

Note that both poems demonstrate close to perfect full rhymes in the final stanzas (perhaps with the exception of 'Emperor/floor', depending on accent), arriving at a resolution in form that complements the coherence of ideas.

Micro to macro

The end-point of each poem can be linked to scrutiny of rhyme schemes and their function in the poems more broadly. 'Sailing to Byzantium' ties the place firmly with art and eternity, as the bird sings:

> *To lords and ladies of Byzantium*
> *Of what is past, or passing, or to come.*

The pairing directly associates the cycle of time and the location through sound in the rhyme of 'Byzantium' and 'to come', and marks their connection through their sequence as a couplet.

Where 'Sailing to Byzantium' uses the couplet traditionally – to mark closure (just as the close of an act is marked in Elizabethan and Jacobean drama) – 'Byzantium' uses couplets as the normative formula (stanzas begin *aabb*), then deviates to a *cddc* pattern. I have already noted the phrase 'death-in-life and life-in-death' as the most overt statement in the poem of a cycle where beginning and end are mutually embedded, where the states coexist at all times. Also described above are the cross-currents through verses, where words and phrases are repeated, echoed, and gently varied (further instances include Hades across stanzas two and three; complexities one, two, and four – and then complexity in five; the moon in one and three; mire in one, three, and five). In combination these bind the poem into an inextricable whole. It thus seems that the rhyme scheme is more than chance, for it manifests similar embeddedness. Given that repeated couplets are the norm in the first half of each stanza, the break in the pattern is noteworthy and the second half can be viewed as one stanza embedded in another, a beginning and an end embedded in another beginning and end. The form internal to stanzas manifests a cycle, consistent with the cycles described verbally and also conveyed through patterning of vocabulary across the poem as if to defy the comparatively simple narrative progression from one stanza to the next. Locating the stanza describing the golden bird at the poem's heart – superfluous to the limited action of the poem – subverts interpretation of the final stanza as the definitive resolution of the poem. Indeed, the transcendental power of art can be identified at the start (the disdaining 'moonlit dome'); here in the middle; and at the end ('the smithies break the flood'). True to the power attributed to the golden bird and hence art to sing 'of what is past, or passing, or to come', this poem assimilates all stages in the cycle concurrently, and has moments of significance throughout. It enacts its own 'images that yet / Fresh images beget', echoing in structure the ebb and flow of the sea and its resistance to easy containment.

Conclusion

Easy containment of these formal characteristics is difficult to achieve, and harder still to teach. Prior to reading the poem with a class, I would identify instances of repeated phrases typical of those I would like students to note, share a couple of examples, and foster discussion about the effect and possible purposes of such patterning. I would seek examples that differ in nature, such as 'flame' where its repetition clusters in a single stanza (perhaps three times in four, to suggest its intensity) as opposed to 'complexities'/'complexity' distributed across the poem and in all but one stanza.

My overarching aim is to help students articulate the effect and meaning-potential of items, so examples must be provided that highlight for students the range of functions each type of patterning can perform. A teaching sequence might begin with consideration of the phrase 'death-in-life and life-in-death', inviting students to speculate on its meaning. It is relatively easy to introduce the concept of embeddedness through this single contained example. Beyond that, students can be guided to find complementary treatment in a form with varying degrees of direction. It may suffice to ask students if they can trace this idea of one thing embedded in another in a) the use of repeated words; b) the use of rhyme scheme; and c) stanza organization. Where I judge more support is needed I give a more overt steer, for example:

> *Stanza three describes the Golden Bird. It is at the heart of the poem. Can you suggest any ways in which this links with the phrase 'death-in-life and life-in-death'?*

Once I feel the exploration is complete, I can return to 'Sailing to Byzantium'. We might begin again with a simple question that promotes comparison:

> *In 'Byzantium' we established that form reflected ideas in the poem. Do you think Yeats's use of form here in 'Sailing to Byzantium' is as important to the communication of ideas as it is in 'Byzantium'?*

The skills developed around the first poem can be applied with a new perspective, and the task laterally supports attention to artistic development too.

Chapter 6

Head and heart: 'No Second Troy' and 'A Prayer for my Daughter'

Introduction

Poet Philip Larkin used an analogy to describe the work of poems that has been much repeated. He saw poetry as performing functions akin to knife and fork together: it can be both sharp and incisive, analysing ideas or experience, and can offer emotional sustenance, nourishing our being.

Examiners' reports on students' answers to poetry papers frequently lament the lack of penetrating or even useful analysis. Students tend to spot various poetic techniques rather than comment on their effects. Students might, on the other hand, pay little heed to the details in the study poems, offering instead subjective and speculative interpretations that might well demonstrate emotional engagement but take early leave from the words on the page.

Inclinations to go in one direction or the other might be triggered by the nature of the poems presented for study or by the context of their reading. If they are about topics, events, or people that students engage with strongly in affective terms, critical distance may be diminished. In other circumstances, students may be so drilled to apply a sequence of analytical steps (perhaps consistent with a mnemonic) that they forget to take account of their intuitive reactions.

This chapter looks at a category of poetry that is likely to stimulate emotional engagement: those that present portraits of individual characters. To read about them is to react to a representation of another person, and perhaps to the person (or more aptly, persona, because it may be adopted by the poet) who voices the representation.

At the same time I consider the rudimentary resource teachers have to guide learning: their questioning. Bloom's taxonomy (Bloom, 1979; Krathwohl *et al.*, 1971) is especially pertinent since two of its three domains are the cognitive and the affective, with much of its influence skewed to the former. Even in pedagogy, it seems, knife and fork do not always work together as well as they might.

The sample poems as examples of poems about people

The poems for attention are 'No Second Troy' and 'A Prayer for my Daughter'. Though they are both by Yeats, they differ sufficiently to capture something of the diversity of poems that are portraits of individuals. Each is an expression of identity, one concerning a relative and one a friend.

'No Second Troy' is about a longstanding member of Yeats's circle of friends. It was published in 1910 in the collection *The Green Helmet and Other Poems*. The subject of his poem 'A Prayer for my Daughter', published in 1921 in *Michael Robartes and the Dancer*, is clear from the title. Both poems are obviously poems about people in Yeats's life. Each gives us a version of its subject. In this they are unremarkable among the many poems whose subjects are individual people. Typically, indeed inevitably, these poems also have in common a voice, a persona, through which we (readers or listeners) receive the portrait. The person as subject is mediated for us by the voice of the poem, in many cases the voice of the poet, though a constructed one. In other poems it may be an adopted perspective, and in yet others the distinction may be blurred. Whatever the type, we are likely to form an emotional or evaluative response to the subject character, and we also have a response to the persona who voices the poem for us, whether we recognize it or not. There are then three identities in interplay in such poems: that of the subject, that of the poem's persona, and our own. Networks of relationships are created as the poems are heard or read, manipulating heart and head.

Such interplay is useful to acknowledge in any teaching where exploiting affective engagement supports learning, and there is little more direct engagement students can have in literary study than reacting to other, albeit constructed, people. Whatever process is chosen by the teacher, students' awareness of the three-way interplay described here can support attention to the poem's work as a device of presentation and their ability to remark on its craft.

A brief summary of Bloom's taxonomy

Benjamin Bloom and his colleagues set out to classify learning tasks and examination questions 'as a method of improving the exchange of ideas and materials' amongst professional educators and researchers (Bloom, 1979: 10). In particular, the taxonomy they developed was intended to support clarification and 'analysis of educational outcomes in the cognitive area of remembering, thinking, and problem solving' (ibid.: 2). Originally they planned to organize the taxonomy in three domains, cognitive, affective, and psychomotor, but only completed the first two. Of the psychomotor domain they said, 'we find so little done about it in secondary schools or colleges that we do not believe the development of a classification ... would be very useful at present' (ibid.: 7).

The cognitive domain concerns knowledge and developing intellectual skills (ibid.: 7). Bloom *et al.* presented six categories in this domain, and posited progression from the simplest to the most complex, proposing that the simplest categories of thought need mastering before the others can be reached: 'the objectives in one class are likely to make use of and be built on the behaviours found in the preceding classes in the list' (ibid.: 18). The categories are as follows:

1. Knowledge
Recalling specifics and universals, methods and processes, patterns and structures, and settings, 'the recall situation involves little more than bringing to mind the appropriate material' (ibid.: 201).

2. Comprehension
'This represents the lowest level of understanding' where the student knows what is being communicated and can make use of it without linking it to other information or 'seeing its fullest implications' (ibid.: 204).

3. Application
This is using abstractions in particular and concrete situations. Abstractions comprise general ideas, rules of procedures, and generalized methods, and can also include technical principles, ideas, and theories (ibid.: 205).

4. Analysis
This entails working with information to recognize its constituent parts, and articulating the relationships between them. Especially relevant to literary study is that analyses 'are intended to clarify the communication, to indicate how the communication is organized, and the way in which it manages to convey its effects, as well as its basis and arrangement' (ibid.: 205).

5. Synthesis
This draws on a range of knowledge to create new meaning and working information, 'combining them in such a way as to constitute a pattern or structure not clearly there before' (ibid.: 206).

6. Evaluation
This is making judgements about the value of information for given purposes, which may be qualitative or quantitative and are linked with criteria.

This hierarchy is the most pervasive of the authors' theories, though Bloom himself observed that the taxonomy was 'one of the most widely cited yet least read books in American education' (Bloom, 1994). It influences conventions of classroom questioning technique, which often build from closed questioning (where specific items are established or information remembered from a previous lesson) to open prompts requiring synthesis or evaluation. Frequently this progression is associated with differentiation, and the assumption is that the more open questions provide challenge for the most able. But does the sort of thought provoked by poetry correspond to the hierarchy? What sort of thinking can be prompted, and does it have a linear progression? And whatever manner of thought might occur in private reading, is a progression in this sequence apt in wider and social classroom study of texts?

Relevant too in reading poetry is emotional, that is, affective response. The poems considered above show the relevance not only of emotional reactions to depicted individuals, but also of judgements about the behaviour attributed to them. Just as we deal in thought when we consider poetry, we deal in feeling and the heart. Bloom's affective domain is important too, and includes learning objectives that 'describe changes in interest, attitudes and values, and the development and appreciations of adequate adjustment' (Bloom, 1979: 7). It is organized into five categories (drawn from Krathwohl *et al.*, 1971).

1. Receiving phenomena
This concerns the receptiveness of the learners and their willingness to engage with the stimuli or phenomena presented to them. It includes directing attention to a particular item, recognizing the object for focus as distinct from other items (ibid.: 176).

2. Responding to phenomena
This concerns students demonstrating active attention and is connected to motivation, 'satisfaction, an emotional response, generally of pleasure, zest or enjoyment' (ibid.: 179).

3. Valuing
This entails the student displaying a behaviour with sufficient consistency that they can be regarded as holding a value, perhaps manifest in their attitude to an activity or in sustained appreciation of something (ibid.: 182).

4. Organization
This is where the student has to draw on more than one value in response to a situation, organizing values and exploring their relationships. They begin

to build their own distinct value systems through reference to available and differing examples (ibid.: 183).

5. Characterization by a value

The learner internalizes values, assimilating them into their behaviour and action, modifying values in light of experience to create a world view or outlook. Others come to recognize and describe the individual in terms of these values (ibid.: 184).

Segall's notion of texts as pedagogical devices even before a teacher sets to work on them proves useful (Segall, 2004: 492). Assuming we are focused on the text in the first place, a poem directs our attention to internal details according to its resources (e.g. a couplet to provide emphatic conclusion by binding items together through rhyme). Similarly, its resources manage how we respond; for instance, in one moment stimulating images in the mind, or elsewhere working intently on our inner ear. In the poems by Yeats discussed here, texts convey value systems that we can take or leave, depending on our sympathies with the persona. The degree to which we internalize the persona's values is influenced by our ability to maintain critical distance. Whatever position we take, however self-aware we might be, what is our capacity to articulate our position? To take an evaluative stance like this we must synthesize the entirety of the poem, and work in the cognitive and affective domains concurrently. The poem does some of this work for us; for instance, it orders and structures ideas across stanzas or within lines, the form of the poem being a mechanism of thought itself.

Describing a possible approach

I want to adopt a teaching approach that complements the way I conceptualized poems about people earlier in this chapter. I identified the three agents interacting through the poem: the subject, the persona, and the reader (the last representing you, me, or our students). So we can begin by drawing up a list of questions for each one.

The questions demonstrate the scope to ask questions that draw on information overtly stated in the text or on the reader's self-awareness. They draw together head and heart, and combine stages from both of Bloom's domains, cognitive and affective: they should not require adherence to a strict sequence, nor should you need to address every single question, as becomes evident when I apply them to Yeats's poems. Beyond their common interest in Yeats's family and friends, the texts differ markedly and are unlikely to yield answers in the same way.

Questions about the subject

CONTEXT
    What is the world of the subject?
    Where are they?
    When is it?
    What is it like?
    What happens there?

THE ACTIONS OF THE SUBJECT
    What do they do?
    Which verbs are attributed to them?
    What is the effect of their actions?

THE APPEARANCE OF THE SUBJECT
    What do we know of their face, movement, clothing, gait, or gesture?
    Which adjectives describe the subject?
    What do figurative descriptions of the subject's outward appearance reveal of their character?

THE SUBJECT'S PERSONALITY
    What is their temperament?
    Is there information about their emotional state?
    Is detail provided about the subject's thoughts?
    Are specific qualities assigned to the subject?

The second list, about the persona, has parallels and works on similar principles.

Questions about the persona of the poem (its voice)

THE RELATIONSHIP OF THE PERSONA TO THE SUBJECT
    Are there direct statements that reveal the persona's response to the subject?
    What are the persona's thoughts about the subject's actions?
    Does the persona convey any emotion in their response to the subject?
    Does the persona make a judgement about the subject?
    Does the persona appear to value specific qualities in the subject?

WHAT THE PERSONA TELLS US ABOUT THE SUBJECT
    How has the persona organized information about the subject?
    Are some types of information dominant, or some favoured over others?
    Is it useful to classify or summarize what the persona has told us?
    Are there gaps or silences that you would like to know more about?

Is there information to tell us about the context of the persona? This could differ from that of the subject.

Does the persona describe any aspects of its own appearance?

Does the persona describe any aspects of its own character?

Does the persona describe any actions it makes itself?

Does the persona comment on how it is telling us about the subject?

Is the persona self-conscious?

Before we apply the questions to Yeats's work, consider how they relate to Bloom's classification of thought in the cognitive domain. Do they span the categories, or do they apply mainly to just two or three? Further, do any of the questions require responses that work in the affective domain, perhaps concurrently? With respect to your own teaching and questioning activity, consider to what extent the mode of thought required of students is prompted by the question itself, and to what extent it arises as a consequence of the poem.

Applying these questions

Most of the questions above focus on the subject and the persona by drawing on skills matching the earlier stages of Bloom's cognitive domain. To answer them, a reader must find details in the text, and so the questions concentrate first on transparent, overt information. But some questions about the persona demand analysis (to comment on how information is organized), synthesis (to classify and summarize information given), and evaluation (to recognize where there may be silences in lieu of pertinent detail).

The final group, outlined shortly, promotes consideration of the craftedness of poems and the manner in which they shape and manipulate our thoughts and emotions. These questions direct students to scrutiny of presentation, to the artifice of texts. They appear to belong to the cognitive domain, but students need to reflect on how craft may direct our feelings in a certain direction. They need to understand affective traits.

Generic questions will have differing resonance according to the poem for study, as is clear when I apply them to two of Yeats's poems. 'No Second Troy' is a sonnet, compact and concise, while 'A Prayer for my Daughter' extends across ten ten-line verses. This signals a likely difference in the degree of focus on their subjects, and the depth of comment.

'No Second Troy'
Why should I blame her that she filled my days
With misery, or that she would of late

Have taught to ignorant men most violent ways,
Or hurled the little streets upon the great,
Had they but courage equal to desire?
What could have made her peaceful with a mind
That nobleness made simple as a fire,
With beauty like a tightened bow, a kind
That is not natural in an age like this,
Being high and solitary and most stern?
Why, what could she have done, being what she is?
Was there another Troy for her to burn?

We can begin by identifying the context of the subject, though she is not named in the poem. Introducing the poem to students, I defer giving the name of the subject in order to maintain focus on the detail of the text. We assume she is a contemporary of Yeats ('in an age like this') and learn something of her circumstances in the third and fourth lines. She has some engagement with so-called 'ignorant men' and she evidently has the capacity to incite their action, as she has with the inhabitants of 'little streets'. That these people might be moved against 'the great' implies a divided society. She has apparently acted to make the persona miserable (line two), though according to the final two lines she has acted true to her nature, and in the only way circumstances permitted.

Of her appearance, we learn that she is uncommonly beautiful ('not natural') though the simile 'like a tightened bow' invites our own associations. The description, which triggers a precise image, may also point to her character. For me the image evokes warfare, but it is the skilled and graceful engagement required of archery. The fact that this bow is 'tightened' suggests someone ready, tense, potential yet to be realized. We know more about her mental state: that her mind is 'simple as a fire' (intense?), has the quality of 'nobleness' (perhaps to distance it from inherited nobility?), and that nothing yet has brought her peace. We have a triplet of adjectives, 'high and solitary and most stern', which speak for themselves. There is much that can be gleaned, then, from ample direct information about the subject, with the syntax being the most likely cause of confusion at first reading.

'A Prayer for my Daughter', however, yields detail of a different order to 'No Second Troy'.

It is comparably abundant in information about the subject's world, the two opening stanzas sharing the function of exposition:

Once more the storm is howling, and half hid
Under this cradle-hood and coverlid

My child sleeps on. There is no obstacle
But Gregory's wood and one bare hill
Whereby the haystack- and roof-levelling wind,
Bred on the Atlantic, can be stayed;
And for an hour I have walked and prayed
Because of the great gloom that is in my mind.

I have walked and prayed for this young child an hour
And heard the sea-wind scream upon the tower,
And under the arches of the bridge, and scream
In the elms above the flooded stream;
Imagining in excited reverie
That the future years had come,
Dancing to a frenzied drum,
Out of the murderous innocence of the sea.

We know that the girl is asleep in her cradle, and the quirky compound noun-phrases convey the sense that she is ensconced beneath 'cradle-hood and coverlid'. Yet we know more: there is a world beyond that safety, of howling storm and 'the haystack- and roof-levelling wind'. Concrete and proper nouns lend specificity: 'one bare hill', 'the tower', 'the arches of the bridge', 'Gregory's wood', 'the Atlantic': this is a more tangible environment than the world of 'No Second Troy'. And the persona of the poem inhabits this world, walks and prays within it. The different contextualizing work of the poems makes the function of expository detail more evident here, for in this poem the intimacy and strength of the relationship between subject and persona is heightened by their common circumstance. Both must survive their context.

At the literal level, the subject's actions come to little but sleep. When students respond to this 'action' question are they alert to the fact that the actions, appearance, and qualities described are imagined by the persona? Consistent with the form, the persona prays for his daughter's future identity, and so students' sensitivity to conditional verbs becomes important ('May she be …'; 'I'd have her …'; 'May she become …'). Assuming this is acknowledged, there is plenty of detail about this envisaged adult daughter. Pedagogically, it would be apt to direct attention according to the organization the text provides, perhaps asking individuals or selected groups of students to comment on different stanzas. Stanza three, for example, concerns the subject's beauty, five her wished-for courtesy, and eight her attitude to intellectual opinion. Where the poem identifies desirable qualities, each is qualified and explained, so the poem moves markedly beyond portrait to commentary on these qualities and what the persona understands by them.

We know something of the actions of the persona of 'A Prayer for my Daughter' (he walks and prays) and we find strikingly overt declaration of his mental state: 'because of the great gloom that is in my mind'. This is supported by description of his developing thoughts, an 'excited reverie' about her future years, so vivid that they seem to have arrived in the moment. The persona is clear about his wishes for his daughter ('In courtesy I'd have her chiefly learned'); he is forthcoming in opinion ('It's certain that fine women eat / A crazy salad ...'); and direct about the influence of his own experiences on his thinking (stanza six – his own mind has in the past 'dried up' because those he admires have not prospered). He even describes his own relationships, for example, with the 'loveliest woman' who lost all she had (bartering 'Plenty's horn').

The persona of 'No Second Troy' is not so transparent, and we know little other than that he suffered days full of misery and that he questions himself whether he should blame her. In this questioning, persona and form elide. Noticing the self-reproach of this first question, what do the other questions asked by him suggest about his state of mind? The poem is entirely comprised of four rhetorical questions, so the formula is significant. Perhaps the poet does not expect answers?

Introducing the element of craft through the reader's response to the poem

The first two groups of questions used to guide my approach concentrated on details stated in the text. This third group leads students to be more self-conscious. They seek information that will not be found in the text but through attention to our own responses. They require our own reflection about what we have gleaned and how:

WHAT DO I KNOW ABOUT THE SUBJECT?
  How do I know this?
  What would I like to know that has not been presented to me?
  What is my emotional response to the subject?
  What judgements, if any, have I formed of the subject?
  How has the poem shaped these?

WHAT DO I KNOW ABOUT THE PERSONA?
  How do I know this?
  What would I like to know that hasn't been presented to me?
  What is my emotional response to the persona?
  What judgements, if any, have I formed of the persona?
  How has the poem shaped these?

WHAT DO I KNOW OF THE RELATIONSHIP BETWEEN THE SUBJECT AND THE PERSONA?
 What do I infer about their relationship?
 Who do I know most about, the subject or the persona?
 To what extent do I find the subject or the persona credible?
 To what extent do I find the subject or the persona reliable?

IS THE POEM ONLY ABOUT THE SUBJECT?
 Does it concern other people or events?
 Does it seem to explore particular themes or ideas?
 If it explores themes or ideas, how do these link with the subject or
 the persona?

ABOUT PRESENTATION
 Does the persona make overt comment about their action of presenting a
 portrait?
 What are the interesting aspects of the presentation for me?

Applying the questions about the reader's response to a poem

Beginning with 'No Second Troy', I give remarks drawn from my subjective response. The comments are not definitive, and if you were to pose the same questions to a group of students, their responses would differ according to their varying perceptions of the persona.

'No Second Troy'

I know about the subject because the persona of the poem addresses questions to me about her. Through his questions I learn about her actions and character or, more correctly, I learn about his experience of her. From the poem I cannot know the name of this subject, which leaves me curious, and I also wonder how she caused the persona such misery. Perhaps because of this I am somewhat ambivalent to the subject. I find it hard to have a positive response to her, though I do not dislike her. My sense is that she may be cold, an inaccessible and aloof character. No doubt this derives from the impression that she is unattainable for the persona. The poem shapes my response through a sequence of four rhetorical questions. Does this contribute to the sense that the subject is remote? As rhetorical questions, they expect no answer, and the detail we receive is not in the sentence form of a statement, so any information I have is indirect. I think I am also distanced from the subject through her association with classical Troy. Even if she is not of that place, she is other-worldly and out of time.

Of the persona, I know he has experienced misery, that he has an intense interest in this woman, and that he is self-questioning. I think he is in awe of her, and feel that he considers himself inferior or slight in comparison. As a consequence I feel sympathy for him but also some irritation: there is little sense of him challenging the imbalance save for the first question. Perhaps the form of the rhetorical question confirms his position of weakness (he has no answers) and makes readers like myself superior to him too, if we think about the questions and wish to answer him.

Clearly their relationship is unequal. On his part at least it is unhappy, his feelings unrequited. I might think her cruel according to his portrayal, but can't be sure she is aware that she has this effect from the detail provided. I have to approach what he says cautiously, recognizing it may be informed by strong feelings that have no expression to her directly. He seems aggrieved. She is as credible as someone on a pedestal, almost a mythical creature, can be.

The link with the story of Troy suggests that this poem is about more than the subject. Her character and actions are cast relative to a grand narrative and so her life and broader history imbue her story with the traits of tragedy. The final question corroborating the title is of interest. Because there is 'no second Troy' it may be that whatever her noble qualities, the contemporary world differs by not permitting their realization. The poem may be about more than her: it also suggests an era in which noble or heroic actions have no relevance. Last of all, I am interested in the form. Ten lines of ten syllables look to me like an incomplete sonnet, the form – like her noble potential – unfulfilled.

'A Prayer for my Daughter'

There is little to know about the subject beyond her innocence and vulnerability. The baby is inert and inactive, sleeping in her cradle. Everything to know is attributed to her adult self, projected by the persona, hence abstracted qualities dominate the description. Because these originate from the persona, we know far more about him: his values, his beliefs, what he hopes and fears. We also know about his current state of mind, of the 'excited reverie' that precedes quite measured explanation of his conservative hopes for inherited custom and ceremony. The baby girl seems symbolic, vulnerable herself but also expressing the persona's own fragility in the face of forces larger and more elemental than him. The poem seems to be less about his daughter than about his own value-system, concisely expressed in the formula that describes the soul as 'self-delighting, self-appeasing, self-affrighting', and in the same verse the implication that our capacity for contentment is in ourselves, not defined by influences outside us.

Although the description of the soul is brief, the poem is not. Across its ten stanzas it draws out explanations patiently and thoughtfully, often drawing on examples drawn from the persona's life. Most of its stanzas elaborate on the wished-for qualities in detail, often with self-aware comment, such that we learn more about the persona's inner thoughts than the concrete world of the first two stanzas. In this one might regard it and him as a little insular. However, if it suggests on one hand a denial of the world in which he finds himself, on the other it confirms the message of that simple formula: that we shape our own state of being.

Stepping outside the questions

What sort of response to the poem has this third group of questions encouraged? They guide readers to awareness of the form of each poem, combined with awareness of their respective effects. With 'No Second Troy', that may hinge on engagement with the repeated use of rhetorical questions. With 'A Prayer for my Daughter', form differs and has a different impact. It seems to manifest a different emotional state. Whereas the form of 'No Second Troy' conveys frustration and some anguish, this poem is more patient, with comment elaborated more comprehensively across its ten stanzas. Both build from formulae that trigger a voice in the head. We might ask the rhetorical questions of ourselves, while the prayer form requires conscious and deliberate articulation (whether spoken aloud or not) to the relevant deity.

The questions I provided about the poems prompt self-aware thinking about our responses to the text, about how the text guides our thoughts and emotions. They require responses that do something more than react to the concepts presented by the poems. They provoke thought about how these things are presented, and how those aspects of presentation work upon us. They treat the poems as crafted literary artefacts. Yet the metacognitive stance they invoke could not occur without the affective as well as cognitive elements working concurrently.

Conclusion

This is not a critique of Bloom's taxonomy, nor an assertion of a specific strategy or even a set of questions. I hope it illustrates my view that it is possible to design an approach to teaching that takes account of the nature of poems for study, informed by the wider field of knowledge concerning learning. Often, unfortunately, this is characterized and even derided as 'ivory tower' thinking. It is ironic that this false dichotomy of theory and practice is made, since Bloom and his colleagues clearly linked their taxonomy with real examples of tasks used in schools. The approach outlined here presents a view of learning around poetry that recognizes the centrality of literary texts and their distinctiveness to the teaching methods selected, because any text first acts pedagogically by shaping thought and feeling concurrently. The inherent pedagogic qualities of texts require attention alongside the use of more generic guiding principles, whether they are drawn from a well-established theoretical framework such as Bloom's taxonomy or from teaching strategies recommended in a handbook or in official guidance. The latter principles cannot be grafted on to treatment of the former: the two need to be merged to create something new and unique, a bespoke approach suited to the texts for study and, more importantly, to the students in the study group. By combining the two, we will encourage good use of Larkin's knife and fork by everyone.

Chapter 7

Poems of a moment: 'Easter, 1916'

Introduction

This chapter focuses on a poem that could be considered historical. Knowledge of the historical context is essential from the perspective of one understanding of the term: history as the course of national politics. That will be unfamiliar for many students, unless they have knowledge of modern Irish history. The relevant history is also the personal history of Yeats, his biography, given his relationship with the historical moment described and his friendships and enmities with the people involved and numbered in the poem.

'Easter, 1916'

Though about a particular event, the poem wasn't written until September 1916, and only published in 1921 as part of a collection (Michael Robartes and the Dancer).

> **'Easter, 1916'**
> I have met them at close of day
> Coming with vivid faces
> From counter or desk among grey
> Eighteenth-century houses.
> I have passed with a nod of the head
> Or polite meaningless words,
> Or have lingered awhile and said
> Polite meaningless words,
> And thought before I had done
> Of a mocking tale or a gibe
> To please a companion
> Around the fire at the club,
> Being certain that they and I
> But lived where motley is worn:
> All changed, changed utterly:
> A terrible beauty is born.

That woman's days were spent
In ignorant good-will,
Her nights in argument
Until her voice grew shrill.
What voice more sweet than hers
When, young and beautiful,
She rode to harriers?
This man had kept a school
And rode our wingèd horse;
This other his helper and friend
Was coming into his force;
He might have won fame in the end,
So sensitive his nature seemed,
So daring and sweet his thought.
This other man I had dreamed
A drunken, vainglorious lout.
He had done most bitter wrong
To some who are near my heart,
Yet I number him in the song;
He, too, has resigned his part
In the casual comedy;
He, too, has been changed in his turn,
Transformed utterly:
A terrible beauty is born.

Hearts with one purpose alone
Through summer and winter seem
Enchanted to a stone
To trouble the living stream.
The horse that comes from the road,
The rider, the birds that range
From cloud to tumbling cloud,
Minute by minute they change;
A shadow of cloud on the stream
Changes minute by minute;
A horse-hoof slides on the brim,
And a horse plashes within it;
The long-legged moor-hens dive,
And hens to moor-cocks call;

Minute by minute they live:
The stone's in the midst of all.

Too long a sacrifice
Can make a stone of the heart.
O when may it suffice?
That is Heaven's part, our part
To murmur name upon name,
As a mother names her child
When sleep at last has come
On limbs that had run wild.
What is it but nightfall?
No, no, not night but death;
Was it needless death after all?

For England may keep faith
For all that is done and said.
We know their dream; enough
To know they dreamed and are dead;
And what if excess of love
Bewildered them till they died?
I write it in a verse –
MacDonagh and MacBride
And Connolly and Pearse
Now and in time to be,
Wherever green is worn,
Are changed, changed utterly:
A terrible beauty is born.

25 September, 1916

As a poem recognizably of a moment, it has in common with many texts the combination of personal and political histories. Aspects it may share with other works include these:

a) It has sections that have a strong narrative momentum;

b) There are sections that are concentrated around symbols;

c) It contains details that allow some explication of the historical moment;

d) It requires some metatextual understanding;

e) It has a voice that is self-conscious about the form it is using;

f) It recognizes and uses aspects of forms beyond poetry.

In terms of pedagogical judgement, related considerations for the teacher might be, respectively:

a) *How can I help students make sense of the narrative element?*

b) *How can I help students attach meaning to the symbols used?*

c) *What can students draw from within the poem that provides information about the historical moment described?*

d) *What further texts will I select and use with students, and with what rationale?*

e) *What is the persona of the voice and its relationship with the text?*

f) *What are the features of the form, and to what extent is it familiar to students?*

In an overtly historical poem, the voice of the poem may not be involved in the historical event described but instead offer a perspective at some distance from the event. This is likely to be at a remove in time, weeks, months or years after the event, thus remembering or reconstructing. Their own part in the event should not be assumed. The voice offers a perspective on an event, but only one (or some) among many.

a) Narrative
Students generally encounter a poem in its entirety at first. On the page they read it line by line. If they hear it first, it will be uttered and received in time. Either way, students experience the text as a sequence of words, sentences, and stanzas. In seeking to comprehend the text they seek coherence or, by contrast, are alert to incoherent aspects. If students first experience this poem in print, the teacher can exploit stanza breaks to support their comprehension.

An open approach asks students to sum up the focus of each of the four stanzas in a sentence. This helps them distil the verse and identify what is salient. Their sentences permit formative assessment by the teacher: how students have understood each stanza and what, for them, appear to be the pre-eminent details. In a gently scaffolded approach the teacher suggests sentences or words that could be associated with the stanzas. I might choose for each of the four stanzas 'words', 'people', 'stream', and 'sacrifice'. Presenting the words together concurrently and asking students to find the stanza most readily associated with each gives them a limited challenge. Pedagogically I may be satisfied with this if I aim to lay down foci for further attention.

However, if I present 'words' first and alone, asking to which stanza is this term most relevant may elicit some more sophisticated evaluative thought. It is obvious that 'words' are relevant to stanza one, with its repeated 'polite meaningless words', but I may wish to exploit the relevance of words also to stanza four and the statement 'I write it in a verse'. If I intend to foreground the self-consciousness of the poetic voice, the activity could legitimately provoke both responses with scope for students to explain their choices. The distinction between the two activity variations is important, as it illustrates the significance of the teacher in selecting, presenting, and withholding information in order to guide students' engagement to differing degrees and purposes.

Tracing a story in a text affords students a more straightforward and holistic engagement with a poem. In poems that do not present an unfolding plot, invite attention to change (of circumstances, states, emotions). Because of the differing character of each stanza here, the teacher could ask, 'Which stanzas do you consider to have a narrative?', and even ask students to identify a hierarchy according to which stanzas have more or less narrative. The outcome is less important than the process, which should lead students to look closely at each stanza, tracing what narrative elements the stanza has. Stanza one of the poem has a narrative strand suggesting the progress of the persona around a city, meeting 'them' at the 'close of day' as they leave their work desks, passing them in the street while recalling times spent 'around the fire at the club'. Superficially a list of different characters, stanza two presents short narratives about each. Even the brief 'This other helper and friend was coming into his force' offers a story, syntactically suggesting he never fulfilled the potential intimated. Stanza three shifts, interestingly, to the present tense, describing 'change minute by minute', so there is immediacy of development and interesting ground for judging whether the term 'narrative' is applicable. Likewise, the final stanza permits attention to roles ('our part') in a story, or to continuing a tale ('what if ...?'). Precisely because the poem does not fall into a narrative mode, prompting thought about narrative is important, helping students hold on to details, to make sense of elements of the poem while allowing also for uncertainties.

Students' attention is directed according to two simple and generally applicable prompts. First, we asked them to summarize stanzas in a word or sentence or, guiding more precisely, provided our own, mindful of the deliberations they might require. Second, we merely asked which parts of a poem could be considered narrative in character.

b) *Information in the text*

Any poem connected to a significant international historical event may be juxtaposed with other texts, in various mediums. Concentrating on working with information available within 'Easter, 1916', the teacher's research of surrounding events will inform the approach to the poem even without presenting further texts. Students have to know that Thomas MacDonagh, John MacBride, Pádraic Pearse, James Connolly, and Constance Markievicz were protagonists and then martyrs in the rising. Some of this might be surmised by reading the final stanza, where the four men are identified by surname, but their significance may not be clear to students. The teaching task is to help students recognize the exact number of people described in the poem, even if the poem itself does not say for sure which information describes any of the four men named.

An approach to stanza two in which the protagonists are described in turn echoes Rex Gibson's interest in deixis applied to Shakespeare's plays (Gibson, 1998: 84). When students consider *Henry V* in print and focus on the scene where the king confronts those that have betrayed him, it is less than clear to whom he is referring, especially when there are no stage directions. Deixis literally means 'pointing out' who is who and naming or labelling them. There may be similar confusion in this poem in stanza two. One by one, five characters are identified, but usually only by imprecise nouns. The voice refers in turn to 'that woman', 'this man', 'this other', 'he', and 'this other man'. The last two or three could be interpreted as being the same person, given the lack of differentiation in appellation. We can only surmise that 'he' differs from 'this other' because the subjects are separated by a semi-colon, and because four men are named in the final stanza.

The first step with students is to help them see how many people are mentioned here. This can be established by didactic explanation. Alternatively, ask them how many people are described, and what they know of each. Even this is quite a challenge, given Yeats's elliptical and figurative turns of phrase. Three traits of the woman described that are readily identified are her 'ignorant good-will', her arguments, and her sweet voice. The first man might be recognized as an ex-headmaster ('kept a school') but that he rode 'our wingèd horse' might puzzle readers who are unfamiliar with Pegasus as a symbol of poetry. A second man is identifiable as the former's 'helper' and 'friend', and a third less for achievements than for qualities ('sensitive', 'sweet his thought') despite his potential having been dashed ('might have won fame in the end').

It is through attention to the qualities of these people that students might note that a fifth person is described, recognizing that the ambiguous 'this other man' introduces another protagonist. That the voice of the poem thought of him as 'a drunken, vainglorious lout' presents a shift in tone, a disruption to the eulogies. In setting up attention to the poem that compels scrutiny of characterization, the teacher leads students to note a disjunction. If they do not ask why there is this inconsistency, the teacher can pose the question and guide them to metatexts. Douglas Barnes gives the term 'differentiated attentiveness' to the varying emphases teachers place on details in the classroom (Barnes *et al.*, 1969: 46). Here, the path of the activity and if necessary the emphatic marking of the distinctive presentation of characters guides students to details the teacher views as helpful to their comprehension of the poem.

The final stanza offers some coherent rationale, some connectedness with previous activity. Having guided students' attention to 'I write it in a verse', and speculated that some of the named men have a connection with the characters described in stanza two, we can promote investigation of the stanza more broadly, asking why the poet writes these names out in verse, and why he draws attention to the fact that he does so. If this question is too open, provide students with items for consideration, prompts around which they can make connections. One can choose direct quotations from the poem: what links can students find between 'a sacrifice', 'needless death', 'their dream', 'I write it in a verse', and 'a terrible beauty is born'? The teaching strategy is to provide cues, giving students the resources to enquire into information that they might otherwise overlook. The teacher creates a situation which increases students' likelihood of finding for themselves an interpretation that correlates with the relevant events of history. This approach maintains the poem as literature, as an aesthetic object, as the predominant focus. The teacher exercises judgement to ensure that in sequence as well as emphasis, attention to the poem comes before attention to metatexts.

c) Information beyond the text

The detail of some poems cannot be understood without reference to information not given in the poem. Students may need to understand the events referred to, the roles of protagonists, or the wider socio-cultural context. Further knowledge might reveal or clarify the perspective on the events in the poem. The historical awareness needed by the reader varies. With 'Easter, 1916', for instance, we might expect students in England, Wales, or Scotland to need more support and direction than their Irish counterparts.

To maintain attention to the detail of the study text, I spend most of the teaching time on the core poem, lest I overwhelm it with extra material.

First, I need to identify what the new details aim to achieve. Some broad purposes are these, illustrated through the example of 'Easter, 1916': I want to clarify the stages of the Rising signalled by the poem's title, what happened on that day, but to do so concisely. I wish to signal some of the causes, but am mindful that they are complex and could distract from the poem and could undermine students' confidence if they cannot grasp them. However, I do need to elucidate some of the poem's allusions, particularly the frequent biographical references. I also wish to realize the significance of some phrases that may appear incidental or mundane to students until they cross-reference them with other sources. Finally, I want to support their insight to the poet's presentation of events and thematic emphases.

To address these purposes requires judicious selection of material and a search for useful resources. The availability of supporting texts depends on the poem to be studied, and texts need to be sufficiently engaging to avoid simply describing additional details to students myself. The time spent on the search should be reasonable, limited to a particular period and perhaps a set range of materials.

To shed light on 'Easter, 1916' I have sought metatexts that can capture the complexity of the Rising with some economy. The National Library of Ireland's collection on the Rising offers letters, books, photographs, and drawings that bring events to life through individualized accounts and records in various modes. I identified appealing visual resources and concise or abridged verbal texts which provide key information that remains intact despite substantial redaction of the documents.

I soon found that a handful of texts could do much to clarify events in the Rising and enhance understanding of the poem. The facsimile of the 'Proclamation of the Provisional Government of the Irish Republic' (Figure 1) is a key resource. It is in the form of a bill poster, and the signatories Pearse, Connolly, and MacDonagh are as clear as they are in the poem. In addition to the visual immediacy, the text clearly signals the impulse for the Rising: 'Ireland, through us, summons her children to her flag and strikes for her freedom'. It declares rights of sovereignty and civil liberty with a strong egalitarian emphasis, and concludes by invoking 'the readiness of its children to sacrifice themselves for the common good' as the nation moves towards 'its august destiny'. The single-page document is a gift for the teacher of 'Easter, 1916': it encapsulates the revolutionary fervour of the Rising, explains the poem's phrase 'changed utterly', and suggests the possibility of martyrdom for the national interest paralleling a concern of the poem that needs to be put into context.

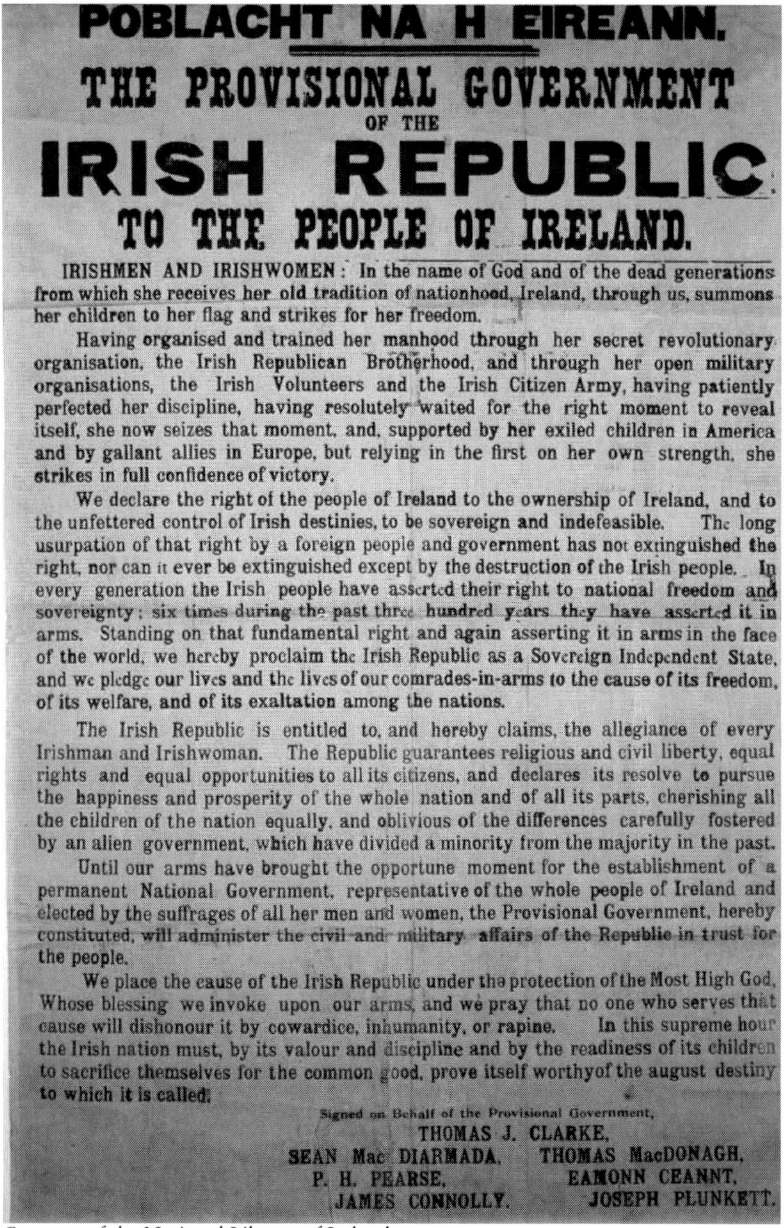

POBLACHT NA H EIREANN.

THE PROVISIONAL GOVERNMENT

OF THE

IRISH REPUBLIC

TO THE PEOPLE OF IRELAND.

IRISHMEN AND IRISHWOMEN: In the name of God and of the dead generations from which she receives her old tradition of nationhood, Ireland, through us, summons her children to her flag and strikes for her freedom.

Having organised and trained her manhood through her secret revolutionary organisation, the Irish Republican Brotherhood, and through her open military organisations, the Irish Volunteers and the Irish Citizen Army, having patiently perfected her discipline, having resolutely waited for the right moment to reveal itself, she now seizes that moment, and, supported by her exiled children in America and by gallant allies in Europe, but relying in the first on her own strength, she strikes in full confidence of victory.

We declare the right of the people of Ireland to the ownership of Ireland, and to the unfettered control of Irish destinies, to be sovereign and indefeasible. The long usurpation of that right by a foreign people and government has not extinguished the right, nor can it ever be extinguished except by the destruction of the Irish people. In every generation the Irish people have asserted their right to national freedom and sovereignty; six times during the past three hundred years they have asserted it in arms. Standing on that fundamental right and again asserting it in arms in the face of the world, we hereby proclaim the Irish Republic as a Sovereign Independent State, and we pledge our lives and the lives of our comrades-in-arms to the cause of its freedom, of its welfare, and of its exaltation among the nations.

The Irish Republic is entitled to, and hereby claims, the allegiance of every Irishman and Irishwoman. The Republic guarantees religious and civil liberty, equal rights and equal opportunities to all its citizens, and declares its resolve to pursue the happiness and prosperity of the whole nation and of all its parts, cherishing all the children of the nation equally, and oblivious of the differences carefully fostered by an alien government, which have divided a minority from the majority in the past.

Until our arms have brought the opportune moment for the establishment of a permanent National Government, representative of the whole people of Ireland and elected by the suffrages of all her men and women, the Provisional Government, hereby constituted, will administer the civil and military affairs of the Republic in trust for the people.

We place the cause of the Irish Republic under the protection of the Most High God, Whose blessing we invoke upon our arms, and we pray that no one who serves that cause will dishonour it by cowardice, inhumanity, or rapine. In this supreme hour the Irish nation must, by its valour and discipline and by the readiness of its children to sacrifice themselves for the common good, prove itself worthy of the august destiny to which it is called.

Signed on Behalf of the Provisional Government,

THOMAS J. CLARKE,

SEAN Mac DIARMADA, THOMAS MacDONAGH,

P. H. PEARSE, EAMONN CEANNT,

JAMES CONNOLLY. JOSEPH PLUNKETT.

Courtesy of the National Library of Ireland

Figure 1: Proclamation of the Irish Republic

A further powerful and useful record from an undated American source, *The Death Speech of Thomas MacDonagh*, provides his statements and those of Pearse before their execution by British Court Martial (MacDonagh, 1920?). The links with the poem are certainly important, but they also have a visceral clarity. Pearse declares: 'to refuse to fight would have been to lose; to fight is to win' and says defiantly: 'if our deed has not been sufficient to win freedom, then our children will win it by better deed'. MacDonagh proclaims his martyrdom as 'the high honor I enjoy in being one of those predestined to die in this generation for the cause of Irish freedom'. Of the proclamation he says, 'in hearts aflame with Ireland's mighty love it was conceived. Such documents do not die'. His speech is found in a book next to an image of the mythic Irish hero Cuchulainn, tethered to a stick in his own defiant suffering. Words and image combine to underline the powerful pull of martyrdom in Irish republican tradition.

Other images convey the architectural character of Dublin. Photographs show the buildings that were the sites of siege or struggle, some damaged in the battles. A photo of the General Post Office makes vivid the location where Pearse read the proclamation. One postcard has the caption 'Royal College of Surgeons where Countess Markievicz surrendered, Dublin', signalling her importance in public consciousness of the events. Both suggest the aesthetic of the city, while a third image conveys more of character and context. Though not a site for events in the Rising, a photo of the Irish Citizen Army outside Liberty Hall (head office of the Irish Transport and General Workers' Union, see Figure 2) provides information about the wider conflict of the Great War in Europe. Over its doorway a banner states, 'We serve neither King nor Kaiser, but Ireland'. The site is captured on a rainy day, puddled cobbles in the foreground. Georgian sash windows and the dreary façade resonate with the 'grey / Eighteenth-century houses' of the poem's opening stanza. Though not apparent in a black-and-white image, knowing that the men wore an 'olive green uniform' sheds light on the poem's refrain 'where motley [green] is worn'.

John Gordon

Courtesy of the National Library of Ireland

Figure 2: The Irish Citizen Army outside Liberty Hall, head office of the Irish Transport and General Workers' Union

Biographical information can be conveyed efficiently too. The Transport Union was led by Joseph Connolly, signalling his committed socialism, and may explain why Yeats describes him as 'sensitive' in nature and 'daring and sweet' in thought. This is reinforced through attention to a songsheet cover entitled 'The Watchword of Labour', which depicts Connolly: he is an individual, not merely a name. A happy coincidence is that the example also indicates the importance of songs as a vehicle for political comment. This could be exploited in exploration of the poem's reference to the oral form: Yeats is conscious of 'the song' (the poem, or perhaps the romantic reification of the Rising) and his creative part in it: 'I write it in a verse'.

Portraits are available for each of the protagonists mentioned: even a simple exercise matching these to the qualities Yeats attributes to each aids comprehension, helping students distinguish between them. Resources available for Pearse clarify relationships: a staff-list from the school he established places him at the top, as Head Master, and MacDonagh as Second Master. It clarifies the lines 'This man had kept a school ...' and 'This other his helper and friend' where names are not provided.

Finally, materials are available that inform our understanding of the poet's presentation of events. The BBC History webpages (see *Resources* list below) provide press commentaries published shortly after the Rising. They signal reservations about the conduct of the insurgency and its legacy. In a piece headed 'The Aftermath', the *Irish News* declares:

> The lives of all these victims 'rebels' 'soldiers' of the Crown and innocent members of the civilian community – will not have been sacrificed in vain if the people of Ireland are wise and brave enough to shape their future course in the light of the lessons that should be brought home to their minds by the catalogue of the week's blunders, disasters, crimes and retributions.
>
> *Irish News*, 4 May 1916

The *Irish Independent* was more direct, heading its commentary 'Criminal Madness', and beginning with the unequivocal 'No terms of denunciation that pen could indict would be too strong to apply to those responsible for the insane and criminal rising of last week'. Making much of the support the republicans received from Germany, it states:

> The men who fomented the outbreak, and all who were responsible for the devastation surrounding us have to bear a heavy moral and legal responsibility from which they cannot hope to escape. They were out, not to free Ireland, but to help Germany.
>
> *Irish Independent*, 4 May 1916

Access to these positions could help students recognize the ambivalence in the poem's refrain 'All changed, changed utterly: / A terrible beauty is born' and in the question 'Was it needless death after all?'

d) *Symbolism and parallelism*

As suggested earlier, stanza three makes rare use of symbolism and is neither readily mined for information nor explained by attention to metatexts. It evokes a mental picture of a pastoral setting alive with movement and sound: 'tumbling cloud', plashing horses with sliding hooves, moor-hens diving and moor-cocks calling, 'minute by minute they live' as part of 'the living stream'. Yet the stanza's last line is 'The stone's in the midst of all', which refers back to 'hearts with one purpose alone /... Enchanted to a stone'. In the fourth stanza 'Too long a sacrifice / Can make a stone of the heart' helps give this meaning. The triangulation affords realization that 'sacrifice' is the means of enchantment to stone.

This approach to study assists students in understanding how the Rising made martyrs of its protagonists, reifying them in the iconographic narrative of Irish independence. One particular detail from the proclamation is helpful: 'in every generation the Irish people have asserted their right to national freedom and sovereignty: six times during the past three hundred years they have asserted it in arms'. Interpretation of 'the living stream' can be expanded beyond the flow of water to the current of history, the rural scene representing the Irish nation.

Stanza four uses the possessive pronoun 'our' to co-opt the reader or listener as participant in a ritual of grief, remembrance, and catharsis, echoing 'Heaven's part' and the role of a mother to 'murmur name upon name'. The phrase 'as a mother names her child' appears innocuous, and could easily be missed. In my search for resources to support teaching 'Easter, 1916' I chanced upon a poem by Pádraic Pearse, entitled 'The Mother' (written 1916; see Ryan, 1979: 24), which conveys a mother's feelings about the involvement of her offspring in armed conflict:

> I do not grudge them: Lord, I do not grudge
> My two strong sons that I have seen go out
> To break their strength and die, they and a few,
> In bloody protest for a glorious thing,
> They shall be spoken of among their people,
> The generations shall remember them,
> And call them blessed;
> But I will speak their names to my own heart
> In the long nights;
> The little names that were familiar once
> Round my dead hearth.
> Lord, thou art hard on mothers:
> We suffer in their coming and their going;
> And tho' I grudge them not, I weary, weary
> Of the long sorrow – And yet I have my joy:
> My sons were faithful, and they fought.

In its overt treatment of sacrifice for 'a glorious thing' and in expressing 'joy' and pride that 'generations shall remember' them, the poem offers an excellent counterpoint to stanzas three and four. It supports not only interpretation but can be exploited for analysis of style. Its intimate first-person voice contrasts with the rhetorical yet imprecise source of the persona of 'Easter, 1916'.

e) Voice and form

My first instincts were to treat 'Easter, 1916' as a poem of the page, as the approaches I have described assume this. It is dense in biographical detail, description of locations, in symbolism, and abstract nouns that suggest it requires lingering scrutiny and analysis.

Students also need to be aware that the voice of the poem varies its register across the poem: what registers are employed, and what do they suggest of the voice's attitude to what it describes?

The poem begins in the first person, recounting apparently mundane matters in a self-deprecating manner. The persona acknowledges his own 'polite meaningless words' and his wish to 'please a companion'. It moves to the highly personal, describing the fifth character as one 'I had dreamed / A drunken, vainglorious lout'. He speaks of John MacBride, married to and then divorced from Yeats's paramour Maud Gonne. This explains the observation that 'He had done most bitter wrong / To some who are near my heart'. In the same stanza the voice becomes self-conscious about communicating with us ('Yet I number him in the song') and about constructing a grand historical narrative. In telling that MacBride 'has resigned his part / In the casual comedy', Yeats implies that the story form has transformed into tragedy. Even from Yeats's subjective and biased viewpoint, events have moved beyond the tangled matters of personal affairs to a new and national scale. The voice now allows that even MacBride has 'changed in his turn, / Transformed utterly'.

The first person is hidden across stanzas two and three, coinciding with the most symbolic sections, which treat the martyrdom in abstract terms. It is as if the voice, like the martyrs, becomes transcendent. In the final stanza, however, the transparent voice returns, drawing attention to the work it is doing. It declares its action and is performative ('I write it in a verse'), naming and enacting the transformation of MacDonagh, MacBride, Connolly, and Pearse into figures of legend 'now and in time to be'.

The simplest means to guide students to this variation is to offer a double-headed arrow, labelled 'personal voice' at one end and 'transcendental voice' at the other, and then request that they organize the stanzas relative to it. They would need to discuss their choices of sequence. And why does the voice draw attention to vocalizing and composing the poem? The voice, a persona of Yeats, is self-conscious about its role singing and writing history. When 'Easter, 1916' is used as a key text, that concept enhances the appreciation of the role of his poetry in contributing to the conception of Irish national identity.

Resources
The National Library of Ireland, The 1916 Rising: Personalities & Perspectives, online exhibition:
www.nli.ie/1916
BBC History pages, including Easter Rising press archive:

www.bbc.co.uk/history/british/easterrising/newspapers/index.shtml
British Library recording of Bob Geldof reading 'Easter, 1916':
www.bl.uk/learning/langlit/poetryperformance/yeats/poem3/yeats3.html

Complex poems: 'Nineteen Hundred and Nineteen' and 'Meditations in Time of Civil War'

Introduction

This chapter discusses lengthy poems that are complex in form and content and epic in scope. Even university students may have little experience of such texts, especially if their study of poetry at school was built around thematic anthologies. Anthologies tend to compare short forms that lend themselves to study in single lessons and can be read, superficially at least, in a few minutes. By contrast, epic poems require extended reading time, and to read them aloud in full would take up entire lessons.

'Nineteen Hundred and Nineteen' and 'Meditations in Time of Civil War' were published together in *The Tower* (1928), though in reverse sequence to when they were written. The earlier poem was written in the year of its title, and 'Meditations in Time of Civil War' in 1923. I note some of the challenges they and other epic poems present to students, then discuss some generalizable strategies of approach. I attend to aspects specific to the two poems and to the work of Yeats, since I believe that tailored attention is crucial to a pedagogy of poetry.

Orientation in response to the nature of study texts

The length of these poems is an obvious challenge that might intimidate students. Each has six or seven movements, usually consisting of multiple stanzas. One movement alone is likely to match in length and appearance the poetry with which students are more familiar. The poems have no overt narrative development but switch from one focus to another across movements. Further, the stanzas often focus on allusions not pre-empted or explained elsewhere in the texts, which can deter the inexperienced reader.

Both of the poems may seem fantastical: ladies on unicorns arrive late in 'Meditations in Time of Civil War', while 'Nineteen Hundred and

Nineteen' is apparently a series of non sequiturs in rapid shifts from weasels to bees to dancers and dragons, which create an effect of disorientation. These characteristics may be a difficulty if we expect narrative coherence, and the search for coherence is more likely to succeed with succinct poems. If we are open to fluid arrangements and prepared to look to other forms, however, these traits may not be quite so alien.

Non sequiturs and interesting juxtapositions are common in film and promotional music videos, and students might know the work of directors such as Spike Jonze (e.g. *Being John Malkovich*, videos for Daft Punk) or Michel Gondry (e.g. *Eternal Sunshine of the Spotless Mind*, videos for Bjork). Television series from the United States, such as *The Sopranos*, challenge and stimulate audiences for similar reasons (Johnson, 2005: 67). Film directors such as Paul Thomas Anderson have used edits that speedily shift us from micro to macro perspectives, while introducing non-naturalistic detail to otherwise scrupulously realistic narratives. In *Magnolia* the biblical shower of frogs that falls while protagonists sit alone in their cars singing Harry Nilsson's 'One' ('One is the loneliest number that you'll ever be ...') is a memorable and affecting example. It may give students a foothold to know that the poems do not follow the conventions of a story. They are not linear, but rather follow the logic of a short film or video.

To suggest a single approach to such carefully crafted poetry which provokes complex response does both text and reader a disservice. Instead, various orientations can be combined according to the nature of the task and the group of students. The options I describe are broadly text level – that is, they concern the poems in their entirety and structurally, rather than analyses of lines and phrases. My rationale is to prioritize helping students assimilate each text as a whole and provide a foundation for attending to later details not as isolated items but as parts in a whole. These wide approaches include attention to:

- narrative development;
- the structural organization of the poem;
- themes;
- symbolism;
- parallels with other poems;
- the poem as a dramatic arc;
- the poem as development of an intellectual idea or argument.

In practice, the teacher may wish to select items from the list that are most relevant to their study poems (probably only two or three at a time), or to sequence the study according to their own judgements. Alternatively, it may be valuable to allocate different items from the list to different students or groups working concurrently. These can be reported on and synthesized in whole-class activities, and the focus for each group can be allocated according to varying degrees of challenge.

Early in the teaching, it is important to read the text on its own terms, for its own sake, either independently or communally when the poem is read aloud. This gives space for the students to sense the cadence of the text and its sustained patterning, for instance through repetition, echoes, and refrains. Selected images in isolation, or their juxtaposition and sequence may also take effect. Because of the scope of the poems, it may be wise to read them both privately and aloud, to ensure that they are read in their entirety at least twice, and so that their effects can be noticed and felt. This further ensures that students have personal or relatively unmediated engagement to build around in later analytic work.

Narrative

An approach driven by narrative will yield different returns depending on the poem. With poems that have strong, eventful story arcs where cause-and-effect are clear (such as Coleridge's *The Rime of the Ancient Mariner*), a sense of chronology can be developed and recorded in notes or a timeline. In contrast, the two poems considered are gentle in terms of their narrative momentum. The development of 'Nineteen Hundred and Nineteen' at its simplest traces the difference between an earlier time (prior to World War I) and the post-conflict now of the title. Along the way it offers generalizations about the state of the times, the zeitgeist of the poem's present. This is relatively linear in the first movement, less so in the following stanzas, though the two strands remain. The narrative development of 'Meditations in Time of Civil War' is similarly subtle and records no dramatic events. The contemplative first movement considers 'ancestral houses', residences with significance to family histories; the second links these thoughts with Yeats's own surroundings and family home. Later the poem describes this same environment in the midst of the Irish civil war and concludes with Yeats's reflection on his response to these events.

Where narrative development is this sedate, students may need a supporting framework of cues to guide them. The concept of cueing is common in the pedagogy of early reading (see Guppy and Hughes, 1999) but is relevant to later teaching and learning around texts. An orienting cue designed by the teacher for students may be as simple as stating a point of origin; for instance, articulating the inference that in each of these poems the voice is that of Yeats himself (or, more accurately, a persona of Yeats sustained across each poem). It is reasonable to imagine Yeats seated in an armchair or at a writing desk at home. For other poetry this technique can use a formula that summarizes the start and end points of the poem, elaborating on the scenario's basic information with sentence stems such as 'In stanza one he contemplates [insert summary] yet by the end of the poem he thinks that [insert different summary]'. Students then trace the main shifts in thought at points in between, verbally or in writing. An even more directed approach would be to identify a number of stanzas where the teacher sees a change, and to guide students thus: 'There are shifts in stanzas X, Y, and Z. How would you describe them?'

Sequence

Where narrative development is so gentle that it may prove barely perceptible to students, a preferable approach is to look at how the organization and sequence of poems underlines change across the texts. Both of these poems make use of clear structural devices that can be exploited to pedagogic purpose. 'Nineteen Hundred and Nineteen' has six numbered movements though not in a strict formula and with considerable variation. 'Meditations in Time of Civil War' has seven movements, each numbered and titled. A simple exercise around 'Nineteen Hundred and Nineteen' is to remove the titles from each movement and ask students to suggest new ones. Looking at the poem together with 'Meditations in Time of Civil War' provides a convenient model in teaching. Suggesting an alternative title requires students to synthesize each stanza and work through a thought process that is both selective and summative.

When seeking to summarize and classify each component of these poems, it may be of interest that they are structured across three levels superordinate to attending to individual lines: the levels of whole poem, movement, and stanza. In my work with A-level classes I found it preferable with 'Meditations in Time of Civil War' to guide students in writing summaries of around fifty words for each movement, rather than précising stanza by stanza. That the movements have simple titles signals the concentrated focus sustained through all the stanzas. The activity outcomes are distilled versions of each movement, which indicate to the teacher what students have understood and which details they find significant. In my notes, and later revision support for my class, I distilled the summaries further to between ten and twenty words, but could just as well ask students to do the same. Through this method students arrive at a succinct overview of the development of a poem. Moreover, the ability to present a concise overview is useful for students when writing essays or exams. The skill precludes digressing or retelling at unfocused length, instead demonstrating the analytic skills required.

One strategy doesn't suit all poems exactly, however: 'Nineteen Hundred and Nineteen', for instance, needs a different way of working. Because its movements are less unified around a single item or idea, summarizing each stanza is best done before summarizing movements. Take the third movement, which has three substantial stanzas that intertwine the symbol of the swan with consideration of the soul and then the individual engaged in 'self-meditation'. I want students to recognize these discretely before they provide an encompassing gloss. This principle applies to any poem combining complex ideas in a similar way.

Themes and symbolism

My next two orientations concern themes and symbols, both conventional means of looking at poetry. In most cases involving poetry of the length of either 'Meditations in Time of Civil War' or 'Nineteen Hundred and Nineteen', doing the narrative or structural work first affords students a 'widescreen' experience of them that is more important than when studying a short poem. With a sonnet, starting with the theme often gives the means to engage with the whole poem. Likewise symbols: there may be only two or three employed across a short form. In these poems, which are the length of at least six or seven sonnets, the manifestation of themes or symbols is more diffuse.

After the precise work on the stages in a poem's development, theme permits a broader engagement at text level than symbolism, which is localized, discrete, and contained. Theme and symbolism, however, may not be evoked constantly or continuously, but emerge and recede at various points across a poem. Symbols are likely to be recognizable as intentional by the poet (especially where familiar symbols recur across their work), while themes are perceived and imposed by readers. This means there is more latitude for students to suggest themes, and their capacity to do so will depend on their knowledge of the poem's context, the poet, and allusions in general. Asking them to nominate, say, three themes gives them agency and promotes evaluative attention, but these can be further refined with qualification; for instance, asking them to identify three themes that occur at least three times across the poem.

Studied in the body of work of a poet, similar strategies encourage connections with other poems. Further prompts that require students to connect the immediate themes with details from other poems afford a useful way in, supporting more elaborate handling of the poem before them. In my notes for 'Nineteen Hundred and Nineteen' I highlighted change and decay as themes which we could link to 'Easter, 1916'. Alternatively, as both poems concern solitary meditative men, indeed embodying them as their voice, they have perspectives that correspond with a compact poem like 'The Lake Isle of Innisfree'. The point at which the poem is studied as part of a collection will affect the themes that are nominated. In teaching, then, it is important to be aware of students' susceptibility to the influence of prior discussions and emphases placed on the texts so far or under the teacher's direction. All that went before becomes a tacit cue for the current reading.

I treat symbolism in the context of a long poem in relation to the film work of Paul Thomas Anderson. This is not because of particular symbolic images he employs, but for his almost instantaneous combination of micro and macro details. *Magnolia* includes a sequence moving us from the sight of a cancer patient resting in bed to a close-up of his mouth, and then to a close-up of cancer cells as if seen through a microscope. The vantage point shifts rapidly, significantly altering our perspective as it relates to scale. This technique is fairly commonplace in film now but was striking then. In poetry we see the same in Simon Armitage's 'Zoom!' (1989). Often Yeats's work gives me the same feeling: the concurrent micro- and macro- levels, that sense of getting minute attention to detail and omniscient revelation simultaneously. Emily Dickinson summed up the effect in a private letter: 'If I feel physically as if the top of my head were taken off, I know that is poetry'.

Yet the power of that effect can depend on the teaching sequence opted for by the teacher beyond the poem in question. The symbol of the swan in 'Nineteen Hundred and Nineteen' is found in numerous other poems by Yeats, including 'The Lake Isle of Innisfree', 'The Wild Swans at Coole', and 'Leda and the Swan'. The impact of the swan symbol when encountered in 'Nineteen Hundred and Nineteen' depends on how the symbol has been discussed and understood previously and on the cues the teacher chooses to reactivate memories of those earlier treatments. In a scheme of work for classes, a teacher could present 'Nineteen Hundred and Nineteen' movement III as if it were a discrete poem alongside 'The Wild Swans at Coole', to prefigure reading of 'Nineteen Hundred and Nineteen' in its entirety, because the depth and extent of the swan symbolism offers the closest parallels with poems described in the present book. In both, the swan is a symbol of the soul defying age and the elements, and embodies a vigorous reaction against nihilism.

In 'Meditations in Time of Civil War' Yeats cues the symbols for us in movement titles, so the approach might be to allocate one movement per group of students and task them with tracing the significance of each symbol by finding parallels in other poems. This poem in particular signals why attention to the long poem may come late in the sequence of study: so much of it can be elucidated by what has been covered previously. The fifth movement entitled 'The Road at my Door' shares with the first movement of 'Nineteen Hundred and Nineteen' description of immediate and local military presence; the first ('Ancient Houses') recalls both 'A Prayer for my Daughter' and 'In Memory of Robert Gregory' in their exploration of monuments and time. The micro/macro juxtaposition is exemplified in movement VI of 'Meditations in Time of Civil War' ('The Stare's nest at my Window') in which Yeats invokes bees to 'come build in the empty home of the stare' through this refrain.

Cited by some critics as symbolic of the soul, the bees also resonate with 'The Lake Isle of Innisfree' and the orderly care of the bees in that protagonist's benign island existence. This is a shocking inversion: beseeched by Yeats, bees 'build in the crevices / Of loosening masonry' amid decay, their activity symbolic of nature's continuing creativity in the midst of brutal, uncertain times. Cross-references aside, the image of the bees through the mnemonic of refrain dwells in the mind like a close-up, a contrast with the sweeping breadth of 'Ancestral Houses' but the culmination of progress from houses in general, to his house, his table, his descendants, to the road to the door, to this specific detail of place. Understanding the symbol depends on the context, the pathway to it.

The emotional arc

Considering poems according to the emotional arc they convey corresponds to what is enshrined in conventional analysis of poetry as *tone*. The approach is well suited to texts that do not have obvious development according to action but which instead trace the shift in emotions of a character or the persona voicing the poem. As with any method tracing change across a text, it is useful to work with students to describe the relevant state (in this case of emotion) at different stages in the poem. Demonstrating with 'Nineteen Hundred and Nineteen', this is best done by directing students to select from each stanza the line which for them represents the most heightened state of emotion. For example, in the first movement, this could offer the rueful opening line 'Many ingenious lovely things are gone'; the nostalgic 'we too had many pretty toys when young'; the more knowing 'What matter no cannon had been turned / Into a ploughshare?' – loaded with the benefit and irony of hindsight; the direct and troubled 'Now days are dragon-ridden, the nightmare / Rides upon sleep' through 'but one comfort left' to the resigned 'Man is in love and loves what vanishes, What more is there to say?' Task different groups of students with studying designated movements, tracing the arc stanza by stanza, and sharing their results to see if movements offer differing shifts in emotion.

There is no need to trace development in movement IV – this four-line stanza is itself a direct expression of a shift:

> We, who seven years ago
> Talked of honour and of truth,
> Shriek with pleasure if we show
> The weasel's twist, the weasel's tooth.

This is an opportunity for the teacher, as it encapsulates a shift within a movement and sums up the shift described across the poem. It could be exploited when introducing the poem, to signpost the nature of the shift described across the entire text. More subtly, it could instead be invoked at the conclusion of the activity, to underline the shift that is conveyed. The final movement too is atypical and a single stanza, though longer. This describes a nightmarish vision of violence ('violence upon the roads: violence of horses') and a tempestuous 'labyrinth of the wind'. The direction the teacher gives to students can be guided by the form. Though it does not have stanzas, the punctuation and syntax mark four sections, the first ended by a colon, the second by a semi-colon, the third section commenced with 'And' and concluded with a full-stop, and the final section apparently a sestet with *abcabc* rhyme-scheme. If the teacher identifies these stages for a class, students can approach the other movements in a similar way. The variations across the poem allow the teacher to apply a simple, generalized strategy of approach while at the same time being alert to the way in which the text changes in details that need special consideration. The nuanced variation of the final stanza can be exploited too as a means of attending to form: why is the final movement not divided into stanzas when it remains possible to recognize structural division?

The development of an intellectual idea or argument

To recognize developing intellectual ideas is immensely challenging and draws on elements of the methods described above. The ideas developed in a lengthy poem are complex and some important aspects defy paraphrase, as poetic expression extends beyond semantic uses of language.

When I prepared to teach 'Meditations in Time of Civil War', I worked through the processes of selection I have described above, until I distilled the poem to a prosaic summary, as follows:

Table 8.1

Movement	Simple summary
I	Yeats contemplates the glory of monumental ancient houses
II	… developing the idea that they will decay by linking them to his own surroundings. He suggests it is his (and any artist's) role to create symbols that transcend time.
III	The sword, like the tower, is such a symbol.
IV	Yeats considers his own heirs and legacy. These represent the poem's most positive monument in the face of change.
V	Shift in tone: Yeats turns to thoughts of civil war in the 'cold snow of a dream'. Ironic that the war is a violent reality. Yeats continues contemplating …
VI	Yeats realizes the uncertain and violent nature of the times and calls for regeneration through the symbolism of bees and their activity. This is the poem's clearest use of placing two contrary ideas together.
VII	Yeats is witness to three phantoms of the blind terror to come. He concedes practical defeat, and consoles himself in the artistic contemplation of daemonic images.

This reductive chart is a guide to my pedagogic approach. It is difficult for students to find a way through the poem to arrive at a summary of its shifting ideas. By working through this process myself I can provide them with prompts to aid their explorations. They are likely to have different interpretations and may develop their own theories of the argument of the poem, so my support may not lead to fully resolved conclusions. However, I can supply leads towards an overarching view of how the poem develops ideas by suggesting the following items to be traced:

Growth and decay
Transcending time
Violence and peace
Artistic achievement

It is then simple for the students to begin with one of these leads and trace details relevant to each movement, recording these by highlighting the text, using flow-charts, or gathering quotations.

Providing terms of reference is what Basil Bernstein (1973) called 'framing'. Bernstein warns that framing that is too strong verges on prescription and could deter students' engagement with the concepts to be learnt or the material presented. The strategy described depends on the teacher's interpretation of the meaning of the poem. I can provide weaker framing, refraining from listing the relevant concepts and instead asking students to develop their own and share them with the class. Once you have a list it can function as a hierarchy. Say students identify ten ideas in the poem: they can arrange them according to which they consider most dominant, either individually or together. Even if the activity is based on the teacher's list, the exercise demands thought and evaluation.

Students also need to articulate how the ideas are explored across the poem, and explain how ideas are developed across the text. Guidance can be formulaic: if the students can identify at least three instances in which an idea is explored in the text, they are in a position to describe development from one example to another. If they can express how an idea is introduced and convey how a second treatment offers something different, they grapple with change. If they can identify a final, concluding treatment of the same idea, they may come close to showing how the poem conveys a position on the matter.

Another strategy is to set these explorations against other poems; ideally another in which the poet explores the same idea in less developed form or taking a different perspective. Prompts based on articulating the different treatments they find can help students deal with the nuance of the poem under scrutiny. When introduced with care, draft versions of the same poem could be presented for similar purpose. If students do not know which is the final published version, they can be asked which would work best at exploring the idea. If there are no connected works, the teacher could bring in the work of a contemporary poet. Ideally the position may differ, but if not, the differing voice or style can help students distinguish aspects of the core study poem.

The final technique invites students to select part of the poem (up to a full stanza) that they feel best captures the essence of the whole text. Explaining how a section presents the heart of a text forces students to pay attention to the unchosen sections too, and to dig out inferred and layered meaning.

Conclusion

The two poems studied in this chapter particularly illustrate how inappropriate generic strategies of teaching poetry can be. Each poem is expansive and challenging, so the detail of the poems cannot be addressed if teaching is then reduced to generic steps. The chapter suggests ways of helping students probe the texts, gradually building their capacity to articulate the thematic interests of each poem, see progress in content from one stanza to another, and find entry points where expectations of linear development may be confounded. Aspects of approach that can be applied elsewhere and to other poems tend to be based on simple reading pedagogy. It is down to the teacher to recognize how different types of cueing might work, and to map their own understanding of complex works before presenting them to students.

I have also suggested how the context for study influences the interpretations of individual poems. Whatever has been taught in the same unit of poetry could have a bearing on the students' readings. The next chapter considers how to plan a sequence of teaching so that the links and differences between poems are optimally exploited to aid students' understanding of texts looked at not only discretely, but also as a collection.

Chapter 9

Poems in sequence: Teaching an anthology

This chapter is about a large group of poems rather than just one or two. It considers planning how to teach a selection of texts in sequence, during several sessions and many weeks – what teachers call a scheme of work over up to half a school term. An equivalent in further or higher education is to plan the sequence of teaching for a module over a semester of around ten weeks.

Once our attention goes beyond individual texts, the links across the group of poems becomes important. Any collection offers numerous options for sequencing, and the poems in the group could be covered even in an arbitrary order. This chapter, however, articulates the sort of thinking and decision-making that goes into designing a sequence of sessions. How can the teaching sequence maintain coherence even where texts appear distinctive and have no obvious connections? How will the order in which students encounter the study texts develop their understanding and growing confidence with the poems? What choices are open to the teacher, and are there principles that can inform the planning rationale whatever the content of the texts?

The material for scrutiny is the material of the book. In eight chapters I have presented eleven poems for consideration but commented in only three on links between the poems, and then only those presented in pairs. Here I look at the poems collectively, proposing that they be taught in the sequence followed in this book:

1. 'The Lake Isle of Innisfree' (1893)

2. 'The Song of Wandering Aengus' (1899)

3. 'The Wild Swans at Coole' (1919)

4. 'The Second Coming' (1921)

5. 'Sailing to Byzantium' (1927)

6. 'Byzantium' (1933)

7. 'No Second Troy' (1910)

8. 'A Prayer for my Daughter' (1921)

9. 'Easter, 1916' (1921)

10. 'Nineteen Hundred and Nineteen' (1928)

11. 'Meditations in Time of Civil War' (1928)

This order (with dates of publication in brackets) is not a correct or definitive sequence, but I can explain my rationale. Connections across the poems are discussed in terms of three strands: their content, craft, and context. I go on to comment on the bearing of connections on students' engagement with the study texts, their development of responses to the poems in isolation and as a body of work, their increasing autonomy of response, and their evolving skills of critical analysis. Much of this is about how to structure the sequence to support the learner's confidence. Decisions the teacher makes at this stage can help plan out difficulty for learners and plan in opportunities for cumulative understanding of the texts, mitigating some of the challenges posed by the most complex poems in the collection. At the same time, the sequence can help students see characteristics shared by the group of texts but also to notice important contrasts, shifts, and dissonant elements.

Content

Discussion of this strand explains how the teaching sequence derives from the content of the study texts. What connections are there across the ideas or narratives of the poems that inform the order in which students read them? On what basis are those elements organized, and why might the teacher find the sequence constitutes a progression of sorts?

The sequence begins with 'The Lake Isle of Innisfree' because it describes a single moment of thought in a clear and obviously subjective first-person voice. Through repetition it is clear that this is intended, the draw of the island vividly described. Several aspects prefigure features that are explored in later poems in the sequence. The persona is an isolated individual, eager it seems to embark on a solitary creative existence. And the poem evokes a pastoral idyll humming with sound. Bees and birds recur in the sequence of poems, as does the lakeside setting. The poem's title states the location, which is specific, real and clearly Irish, thus anticipating direct evocation of Irish locations. As well as the rural scene, the Dublin cityscape is evoked, as it is in 'Easter, 1916'. The poem's final line, 'I hear it in the deep heart's core' indicates the subject's instinctive and compelling yearning, articulating emotion and motivation that is more than mere rationalism.

In this the poem anticipates 'The Song of Wandering Aengus', which evokes a liminal state and then reverie. Both poems suggest hazy conditions, though at different times. The first has midnight 'all a glimmer' and 'noon a purple glow', and in the second 'moth-like stars were flickering out'. Although vocabulary is echoed with 'glimmering girl' we can see that the persona's perception of the environment is more fully merged with phenomena in it. The state of tranquillity and accord with the natural world described in the opening poem is followed in the second by a supernatural yet equally vivid real encounter. The persona's rural existence is indicated in tangible items: the crafted ('cut and peeled') hazel wand, a necessity like Innisfree's cabin of 'clay and wattles made'. The content has developed, since 'The Song of Wandering Aengus' makes overt Yeats's interest in folkloric narratives and Irish faery legend. The sudden disappearance of the girl and Aengus' lifelong search for her manifests yearning again, a search for something ethereal and unattainable beyond rational sense. This state of being is articulated in a distinctively Irish form. The journeying and its correlation with ageing looks ahead to 'Sailing to Byzantium', but before that we consider 'The Wild Swans at Coole'.

The first three poems are all representations of Ireland. Innisfree is a real place recreated in the persona's mind; the scene of 'The Song of Wandering Aengus' is an archetypal setting of Irish legend, and Coole Park is a significant place in Yeats's autobiography, invested with the spirit of a friend. This last poem in the triplet has a more direct grounding in actual and empirical experience. The persona's observation of the swans moving around the lake is the trigger for contemplation, whereas the other two poems express intentions or describe remembered events. Nevertheless, existential yearning is apparent here too: 'I have looked upon those brilliant creatures / And now my heart is sore'. 'The Wild Swans at Coole' continues the interest of 'The Song of Wandering Aengus' in the process of ageing but defies the passage of time ('their hearts have not grown old'). At the same time it sustains reference to birds (linnets in 'The Lake Isle of Innisfree', more swans, golden birds, and falcons to follow) and introduces a motif of circular movement ('great broken wings') that anticipate the gyres of 'The Second Coming', but in an organic, inobtrusive manner.

I have already discussed the connections between the next pair of poems, 'Sailing to Byzantium' and 'Byzantium'. What do they add to the developing sequence? They move beyond Ireland, signalling to students that Yeats's poetry is not parochial or limited in scope. The poems about 'Byzantium' provide a vision of a culture where art and craft are prized: values linked by Yeats in other poems to Irish national identity. They also sustain 'The Wild Swans at Coole's' themes of ageing, death, mortality, and, by implication, their opposite. These themes are drawn together with artistic achievement in the symbol of the golden bird, which sings across the city and down through time: it is possible for human endeavour to find approximation to immortality. Supernatural and spiritual phenomena are introduced, though the presentation differs from the magical charm of 'The Song of Wandering Aengus'. The spirits are anonymous and more mysterious, hinting at forces beyond their own manifestations. It seems right that students encounter the supernatural first in the accessible shape of the musical versions of 'The Song of Wandering Aengus', prior to this more ritualistic event.

The Byzantium poems shift the location of the poetry away from Ireland and to the east, to the Asiatic, as does 'The Second Coming'. While the Byzantium poems maintain specificity in location, 'The Second Coming' brings a new vagueness that suggests imminent apocalypse. I delayed its introduction because of its difficulty for students to grasp but now, I hope, experience of other poems will offer them footholds. The gyre movement of the falcon echoes that of the Coole Park swans, and their 'broken rings' resonate with the fact that the 'falcon cannot hear the falconer'. Both share an intimation of unease: something is not right. This poem's allusions, for example, to *Spiritus Mundi*, have a context in the spiritual encounter of 'Byzantium'. The unleashing of overt violence ('the blood-dimmed tide is loosed'), such that progression from the relatively light, even whimsical mood of the first couple of poems to an altogether darker tone is apparent. Students have, however, seen 'Byzantium' and while history is relevant within the Byzantium poems, this sequence indicates to students the breadth of Yeats's interest in time: the sequence spans ancient civilizations up to contemporary Ireland, enabling the teacher to explore the cycle of 'twenty centuries' and time in units of millennia rather than moments.

The next poems in the sequence are linked more with Yeats's personal relationships but retain comparable sweep. 'No Second Troy' presents his friend and lover Maud Gonne in the context of Greek myth (though he undercuts this mythologizing in the title), while in 'A Prayer for my Daughter' he seeks to protect his child from the howling winds that cross the Atlantic – and which summon up the elemental forces of 'The Second Coming'. It is important that this poem be studied after the Byzantium poems. It expresses Yeats's thinking about ceremony and hereditary customs, so the prior exploration of the passage of time and human perpetuity through the arts is helpful.

The poem can also be seen as part of a group in which intimate, even domestic, details are part of mythologizing and highly complex poems that also relate to events specific to Ireland across and after the First World War. The sequence has been designed to recognize these tendencies discretely in the earlier groups of poems, so that students are already familiar with them and handle them with some confidence. They are better placed to consider the relationships between strands within these poems, and to recognize their complexity and craft pulling these characteristics together. Similarly, they will be familiar with a variety of symbols – swans, bees, rivers, lakes, architectural monuments – and they will interpret later poems in light of all they have seen before. Because the final two poems are significantly longer than others in the selection, students need to develop the confidence and mental stamina to approach them. Having considered each shorter poem with care, they can come to the end of the scheme able to respond to each stanza with the same level of attention. Just as they have made connections between shorter poems, they can apply the same skills to recognizing internal connections in the long works.

Of all the collection, 'Easter, 1916' is the most precise in being fixed to a place and moment. It demonstrates the confluence of Yeats's own life with a major historical event, signalled by the poet's acknowledgement of the protagonists and their relationship to him. It too presents versions of Ireland, though without the pastoralism of the earlier poems. There is disillusionment in the descriptions of Dublin that make up the first stanza. The initially familiar rural images of the third stanza, of moor-hens in the stream, and a horse crossing, become symbolic ('the living stream', the flow of time, and nationhood) but for Ireland 'the stone's in the midst of all' and the martyrdom means all is 'changed, changed utterly'. For Ireland, 'wherever green is worn', there can be no return to the pastoral idyll. The relevance of Yeats's wider conception of history is clear in the way 'a terrible beauty is born' echoes 'The Second Coming'. At the same time, this poem sustains the self-conscious recognition of formal precedents evident in both 'No Second Troy' and 'A Prayer for my Daughter'. Yeats repeats again and again the fact of the poem's construction: 'I write it in a verse'. This reflexive aspect therefore comes to the notice of students in the last stages of the teaching sequence.

Though linked to a particular year, 'Nineteen Hundred and Nineteen' is less focused on individual events than 'Easter, 1916'. Nevertheless, it responds to contemporary circumstances and articulates the zeitgeist: 'now days are dragon-ridden, the nightmare / Rides upon sleep'. While some images act as reportage of an increasingly chaotic and violent Ireland ('the mother, murdered at her door' crawling in her own blood), other phrases tie the events to the unspecific yet sinister intimations of earlier poems. This mother was killed by 'a drunken soldiery', the same noun phrase that is found in 'Byzantium'. 'Byzantium' is recalled in 'the barbarous clangour of a gong' which marks a dark rhythm for humanity, also associated with Loie Fuller's Chinese dancers. Their whirling and winding suggests the gyres. With lexis akin to 'The Second Coming', the poem ends in 'a sudden blast of dusty wind', a 'tumult of images', and a fiendish figure (Robert Artisson) 'lurches past'. The poem thus ties commentary on immediate circumstances to the historical perspective presented in other poems, vocabulary binding one to the other.

Similar links apply to the poem's symbolism. The third movement finds the persona explaining the comparison made by 'some moralist or mythological poet' of 'the solitary soul to a swan'. It is an idea students can recognize from 'The Wild Swans at Coole'. The vocabulary of 'clamour' and 'mirror' suggests the connection is more than accidental. The web of connections means that this poem and the last in the sequence communicate not only on their own terms but can be understood better by students because they can be perceived as synoptic summaries of everything that has gone before.

'Meditations in Time of Civil War' brings the sequence full circle in that for much of the poem it adopts a first-person voice that, like the voice in 'The Lake Isle of Innisfree', describes its immediate home. This time the home is real rather than imagined: the ancient tower that Yeats bought, attracted by its symbolic potency and historical interest. In contrast with the first poem of the sequence, however, the use of the setting in the poem is not a romantic idealization. Instead, Yeats's actual home is immersed in the 'living stream' of history referenced in 'Easter, 1916', with soldiers at the door (movement V) and death outside ('somewhere / A man is killed, or a house burned').

Where 'Nineteen Hundred and Nineteen' was unremittingly bleak, 'Meditations in Time of Civil War' offers some hope, and amidst the violence, a mother bird feeds her young and bees 'build in the crevices' while the poem's voice beseeches them over and over, 'Come build in the empty house of the stare'. Other movements recall Yeats's interest in permanence through art and architecture, and 'My Descendants' has connections with the preoccupation of 'A Prayer for my Daughter' with heredity and ceremony. All are combined in the final movement, which in its title shares the disturbing visionary character of 'The Second Coming': 'I see Phantoms of Hatred and of the Heart's Fullness and of the Coming Emptiness'. The first stanza of this section provides an opportunity to support students in finding links with the full sequence of poems studied previously, the resonances many and likely to be apparent to students now that they have explored the poems one by one. The clarity and simplicity to this stanza matches the situation: Yeats represents himself climbing to the top of the tower to survey his surroundings, subject at the same time to visionary perception in which poetic insights familiar to us from the earlier poems combine with fresh images. The 'glittering sword' of the moon and 'glimmering fragments' of mist shape a reverie that recollects the first two poems but this also has the power to 'perturb', 'monstrous familiar images' echoing the darker poems in the selection. Given that these are unspecified, students can make suggestions about the terrifying images Yeats might be seeing. Interestingly, Yeats identifies the play of these images in 'the mind's eye'. These later poems do more than stimulate the mind's eye: this poem also recognizes the working of the mind's eye and describes it. Like 'Nineteen Hundred and Nineteen', this poem is explicit in describing a psychological process rendered in verse, fulfilling a progression to reflexivity evident across the anthology. That development is associated with aspects of craft, the next focus for this chapter.

Craft

Organization according to the content of a group of poems is only one means of sequencing. Depending on the texts for study and the nature of assessment, it may be equally valid to organize material with attention to characteristics of style or form. Many assessment specifications and curricular documents tend to describe these aspects under the term 'the author's craft'. To facilitate students' learning, it is as important to identify connections between poems. It may also be helpful to conceptualize attention to the author's craft, similarly to provide footholds for students so that they can develop their skills of analysis across the scheme. In practical terms, this is likely to mean that we do not expect students to make comprehensive analysis of each poem from the outset, still less that we require them to be able to identify every stylistic feature of every poem in the sequence. As with content, the planning process will entail identifying sub-groups of texts, seeing connections between them, and considering how students' thinking about the author's craft will develop incrementally poem by poem.

Let us take *simile* as an example of a relatively simple poetic device that could well be used in every poem in a sequence. It would be logical to identify the poem that makes most use of simile and use it as the basis not only for exploring use of the technique in the poem but also to help students articulate the workings and effect of simile verbally and then in writing. Once the teacher is happy that students can speak and write about simile with confidence, they can expect to be able to transfer their skills to their attention to other poems, and to do so independently. Progression in their learning means that when the next poem is considered the same level of scrutiny on similes is unnecessary. Instead, the teacher may opt to focus on a poem that makes figurative use of language, but with a different device and with greater sophistication or complexity. Attending to the use of metaphor and then examples of extended metaphor is a natural progression. The skills required to articulate the responses suggested by a single metaphor contained within a sentence or line of verse differ from those required to explain how a metaphor is extended across more than one instance, developing stanza by stanza or image by image. The isolated metaphor requires only one quotation, whereas extended metaphor requires students first to identify the items that trace the extension of the metaphor and, if they are to provide analysis, to mark the development of the concept from one idea to the next while also expressing the coherence of the chain.

This suggests that developing students' capacity to express the workings of the author's craft is time consuming. Different aspects of craft require particular explanations. It cannot be assumed that the same formula works effectively for each technique. The paragraphing formula 'point, evidence, explain' has been widely used in literary analysis but is increasingly subject to variation because it can inhibit subtle response. It assumes that using one quotation will suffice for whatever analytic point a student wishes to make. Attention to extended metaphors is neglected as this requires at least two references to the text. The formula is also likely to restrict attention to word- or sentence-level aspects of text. Unless examples of analysis accommodate more than one example of textual evidence, students are unlikely to offer responses that relate to whole stanzas or entire texts. And some aspects of an author's craft are less readily captured in carefully selected quotations. Those formulae are not much help for students to understand how a poet subverts the conventions of a poetic form, or to explain the narrative or conceptual development of a poem.

With this anthology of Yeats's poetry these matters are important. I may need to find means for students to explain Yeats's idea of the gyres of history, and 'The Second Coming' is the best focus for doing so. I may intend that they develop capacity to highlight instances of gyre-like movement in other poems at the same time, and make concise, judicious reference to their significance. Advanced students may need to write about Yeats's use of symbolism, writing about the use of a single symbol across a handful of poems, possibly very concisely. An obvious example would be Yeats's frequent use of bird symbols and most commonly the swan. I consider 'The Wild Swans at Coole' the best text to use to introduce symbolism. If students understand and articulate the symbolism here, they may become sufficiently independent to explain swan symbolism when it recurs in the sequence, for example, in 'Meditations in Time of Civil War' and, moreover, to express any development or variation in those poems too. Students should learn more than just how to write about swan symbolism, however. They need to apply what they have learnt about writing about a specific symbol to other symbols. When I work with students on 'The Wild Swans at Coole', the objectives include understanding and expressing how the swan symbolism works, but also learning the generic skill of writing about symbolism, to be exercised on other texts and other symbols.

Context

Another rationale for organization of a sequence of poems can take account of the context of their production. At its most straightforward, this would involve organizing the work of a poet in chronological order of composition or publication. This affords attention to the development of a poet's thinking and craft over time, especially when the selection spans a long period over which the cultural and political contexts change. This clearly applies to Yeats. Or poems could be grouped according to the poet's biography. With Yeats, for instance, a group might be linked because of shared reference to Maud Gonne, another group to family and friends, and another to Yeats's involvement in politics.

In the sequence presented above, arranged primarily according to content, there is also progression according to an approximate chronology of Yeats's writing and publication. 'The Lake Isle of Innisfree' and 'The Song of Wandering Aengus' exhibit the influence of nineteenth-century Romanticism. Reading these, it comes as no surprise that Yeats was in this period a great admirer of William Morris. The sequence moves on so that literary influences of Modernism and inter-war culture become apparent. The interest in eastern cultures evident in the Byzantium poems and 'The Second Coming' is illustrative, while the lines 'things fall apart / the centre cannot hold' have become synonymous with the Modernist movement and the end of God after Darwin. The later poems in the scheme chart the upheaval in Irish politics, chronologically in terms of events being the focus for each poem, so that 'Easter, 1916' is followed by 'Nineteen Hundred and Nineteen' and then by 'Meditations in Time of Civil War'. I felt that any other arrangement would create unnecessary confusion for students. Even when the poems are studied in isolation, the events they describe are complex and challenging for students to understand. The events are also interrelated, and students could easily become muddled about the connections between them if the poems were presented in another order.

Fortunately, the selection of Yeats poems used has interesting signposts to his maturing and advancing age. The first two poems convey the idealism and to an extent the sensuality of youth, while 'The Wild Swans at Coole' and the Byzantium poems indicate a removed perspective on the ageing process. In the later poems, we come to know about the poet's parenthood and about his changing relationships with friends and acquaintances. In the more overtly political poems, the voice of each persona tends to maintain an observer's distance, able to recognize the contradictions inherent in each event, for good and for ill. 'Meditations in Time of Civil War' provides some resolution despite the surrounding chaos: Yeats at home in his tower, finding some way to reconcile the chaos of the world with his own experience, and in such a way that he can get beyond the despair that permeates 'Nineteen Hundred and Nineteen'.

That an emphasis on context could complement sequencing these poems according to either content or craft or both demonstrates that the material for study should shape the impulse for organization. The rationale cannot be imported and imposed; it needs to arise from the teacher's engagement with the study texts and their judgement about what manner of organization will be most appropriate to support students and their developing responses to texts. The opportunities and potential emphases will be defined by the body of work. Some collections offer helpful confluence, while others might require more distinct sub-groupings, which could create some difficulty in making connections across the whole collection.

The teacher needs to keep an eye on the skills their students need to develop. These remain consistent across sequences whatever the collection. A continuum of skills can be determined that are necessary for articulating responses to literary texts, and can guide the teacher to ensure students make progress in applying the language of literary criticism to texts. However, the teacher must be judicious. Some poets rely more than others on the potential of poetry to evoke pictures in the mind through figurative language. Manipulation of form or sound may be the favoured resource, in which case the work of the teaching sequence will be to provide both the generic metalanguage and also a vocabulary with which to explain the subtle craft of the poet. Students might require vocabulary enrichment so that they have the adjectives suitable to describe the shifts in tone found in a poem or across an oeuvre. Clearly this will be unique to the collection for study.

These teaching plans acknowledge the interplay of content, craft, and context in the collection of Yeats's poems, and consider how attention to each poem would support progress in each area. The objective is to become sufficiently confident to deal with 'Meditations in Time of Civil War' with some autonomy. With respect to content, they require reading strategies that make sense of the organization, but which also exploit understanding of details 'beyond the lines', that is, information not presented in the poem itself. The poem is not easily understood without knowledge of the context, and though the title is indicative it is hard to appreciate the persona's response without knowing about the Easter Rising. The craft seems to draw on both the range of tone and the variety of symbols encountered in earlier poems, but to present them in an ambitious, expansive form, which could be intimidating if one has no experience of its influences. So identifying the text likely to pose the greatest challenge for students, and considering how other poems for study point towards it, is a useful starting point for any sequence.

Last words

Teaching poetry as the object of literary analysis is complex. This book shows how the teaching of poetry combines a general understanding of learning, reading, literary study, and specialist knowledge of the texts to create something unique on each occasion. Much depends on the efforts of the teacher, and their own deep engagement with the poems. This often necessitates considerable study, including close reading of the poems, familiarity with some aspects of the poet's biography, and an understanding of the historical and literary context for the work.

Resources are available that underpin the teacher's pedagogy and inform the approach to texts. Some of these are outlined below. They provide a good foundation from the start and support flexibility of approach over time.

Recommended texts

Ruth Padel: 52 Ways of Looking at a Poem

Models of literary analysis that are succinct and in a register that is accessible for students are hard to find. Advanced literary criticism abounds, but is often written for experienced academics and not school students. Obviously it is not intended to demonstrate how to write for coursework or examination. One can draw on real examples shaped by students but this cannot convey to students that people engage in such writing outside school. Because Padel's work was originally intended for the general reader, it shows students how to write about poetry in an enthusiastic yet insightful way.

Padel's book gathers weekly articles she wrote for *The Independent* over a year. Each article presents a poem and a three-page commentary. The concision makes it easy to draw on examples over time. By sharing pieces with students for homework, lessons can focus on the relevant poems. Each article could conveniently form the basis of a lesson, but the discussion of them needn't take that long.

Padel's attention to the distinctive resources of poetry is impressive: she explores the working of sound and metre lucidly but consistently articulates their possible effects on listeners and their role in conveying meaning. Students are known to find this balance difficult to achieve, so will benefit from studying these models of poetry analysis.

Peter Abbs and John Richardson: The Forms of Poetry

This book is, on the face of it, a textbook. It is presented as a map of different literary forms of English in poetry, providing detailed descriptions of verse forms, visual poetry of various types, and aspects of metre and syllabification. It discusses patterning in poetry, the matter of voice, response, and feeling, and the appeals poetry makes to the imagination.

Like Padel's book, the work is concise and practical. Each chapter comprises a small number of well-chosen poems to illustrate its focus, carefully staged attention to the core concepts in each area, and tasks that can be presented to pupils. The chapter on 'The voice of poems', for instance, categorizes poems in three groups: conversations in verse, dialect poems, and poems that express the inner voice. Students are required both to make poetry and to analyse it. The chapter on sonnets features a case study of the making of a sonnet, Wilfred Owen's 'Anthem for Doomed Youth', with draft versions reproduced alongside the published text.

Each chapter offers the teacher an excellent basis for teaching the major forms of poetry. It provides clear definitions of each form and an outline of their conventions, examples of texts to draw from, and tasks devised to develop students' understanding. The same principles can be applied to other texts if the teacher amends the activities. The book is a useful template for approaching poetic form.

Attridge and Carper: Meter and Meaning

This book's strength lies in its flexibility. Many dry accounts of metre are available, but few support students' understanding of the characteristics of different metres or their contribution to the sense of a poem. Often these books are prescriptive, telling the reader the correct stress of words in a verse and what the interpretation should be. Attridge and Carper allow for the possibility that anyone who reads a poem for metre will have their own accent and speech patterns so will stress the text in their own way.

They often provide two or more options for stressing the lines in specific poems, and usually invite the reader to test their own utterance against the demonstration examples. Their discussion thus guides the reader towards a self-aware and engaged understanding of metre, such that it cannot be construed as correct or incorrect. Readers can recognize that different patterns of stress may be valid, and reflect on the significance of these differences for interpreting poems. The section looking at Wordsworth's 'Daffodils' (Chapter 4, 'Scanning poems') is especially interesting, exploring the link between the pattern of beats and the movement of the flowers. The chapter, like others, includes exercises that parallel the examples and allow the reader to find the rhythm in additional poems for themselves.

The book is less likely than either Padel or Abbs and Richardson to be of direct practical use in classrooms, but its illustrative examples can be adapted for use in teaching. Most importantly, the ethos can be applied to any poetry presented to students and support the teacher in their handling of metre.

James Fenton: An Introduction to English Poetry

Like Padel's, Fenton's book is a series of entertaining newspaper articles about poetry. It might also be considered a cousin of the Abbs and Richardson book, covering similar territory, although less intended for the classroom. But it can usefully inform the teacher's preparation, with each chapter focused in a way that could be applied to individual lessons. The chapters 'Writing for the eye' and 'Where music and poetry divide' show how attention is given to the modal resources of poetry and the latter chapter also illustrates how Fenton's comment goes beyond the texts to consider the context of their presentation. It outlines the 'traditional means' of oral performance such as raising the voice 'in order to be heard above the crowd' and 'to demonstrate its beauty and power'. Both are consistent with the assertion that 'poetry carries its history within it, and it is oral in origin'. Overall, the book provides a sound basis for the teacher who wishes to enhance their confidence in discussing the many facets of poetry with students.

Paul Hyland: Getting Into Poetry

Hyland's book to be seems aimed at those who would like to write poetry for pleasure or professionally rather than at students or teachers. However, the section mapping the various literary movements and fashions in poetry is extremely useful for late twentieth-century developments and contemporary trends, which tend to be less well served in wider literature than movements such as Romanticism and Modernism.

Hoyles and Hoyles: Moving Voices

For me this is the pre-eminent collection on black performance poetry. It traces the history of the tradition through to the present with examples in text and, true to its emphasis on performance, on an accompanying compact disc.

This combination makes it an ideal starting point for teaching about this tradition, as it provides the materials to draw on and discussion which can inform the teacher's knowledge. It offers a canon of major figures and influential forms, but leaves space for teachers to make their own judgements about how to present the material to their students and with what emphasis.

Sandy Brownjohn: To Rhyme or Not to Rhyme?

Though this is subtitled 'Teaching children to write poetry', it has much wider potential. Like Abbs and Richardson, Brownjohn focuses on poetic forms, providing a description of each with at least one example. The economy is welcome, and the examples are particularly useful for teachers working with younger students in the secondary phase. Because the emphasis is on writing poetry and consistently linked to examples, there is plenty to inform any activity where the teacher finds it useful to engage students in creative work that parallels the approach manifest in the study text.

Ted Hughes: Poetry in the Making

Written in an era when the context for teaching poetry was very different and there was no national curriculum to standardize arrangements, Hughes's work has a different perspective from the others described here. The book was linked to a series of radio programmes intended for schools and is addressed to an audience of children. Hughes's assertion that 'words look after themselves, like magic' (1967: 18) looks today as though it belongs to progressive models of poetry teaching, far from the present official discourse.

Hughes's approach connects with a spiritual and bardic tradition that focuses more on the speaker than the listener, the utterance above the response of those to whom it is addressed. Instinct and spontaneity are prized above systematized teaching methods and the book is organized by theme. Hughes considers discrete groups of poems in each chapter, gathered under titles such as 'Capturing animals', 'Learning to think', and 'Writing about landscape'. In each he expresses how poets might approach a subject for writing, showing their mode of thinking rather than particular steps to be taken. The focus is not on literary reading, though the discussion of how poets (including children as poets) approach their work can be used to support students in developing empathy for the craft of poets and the distinctiveness of the resources they draw on.

References

Abbs, P. and Richardson, J. (1990) *The Forms of Poetry: A practical guide*. Cambridge: Cambridge University Press.

Armitage, S. (1989) *Zoom!* Newcastle-upon-Tyne: Bloodaxe.

Attridge, D. and Carper, T. (2003) *Meter and Meaning: An introduction to rhythm in poetry*. London: Routledge.

Barnes, D., Britton, J., Rosen, H., and the London Association for the Teaching of English (1969) *Language, the Learner and the School: A research report*. Harmondsworth: Penguin.

Bate, J. (2000) *The Song of the Earth*. London: Picador.

Bernstein, B. (1973) *Class, Codes and Control: Vol. 1, Theoretical studies towards a sociology of language*. St Albans: Paladin.

Bloom, B. (ed.) (1979) *Taxonomy of Educational Objectives: Handbook 1, Cognitive domain*. London: Longman Group.

— (1994) 'Reflections on the development and use of the taxonomy'. In Anderson, L.W., and Sosniak, L.A. (eds) *Bloom's Taxonomy: A forty-year retrospective*. Chicago: National Society for the Study of Education.

Bradbury, M. (1971) *The Social Context of Modern English Literature*. London: Basil Blackwell.

British Library (2003) *The Spoken Word: Poets*. British Library Sound Archive CD. London: The British Library Board.

Brownjohn, S. (1994) *To Rhyme or Not to Rhyme?: Teaching children to write poetry*. London: Hodder and Stoughton.

Bruner, J.S. (1966) *Toward a Theory of Instruction*. Cambridge, MA: Belknap Press of Harvard University.

Buell, L (2005) *The Future of Environmental Criticism: Environmental crisis and literary imagination*. Oxford: Blackwell Publishing.

DfEE (2000) *The National Curriculum*. London: DfEE/QCA.

Dorn, E. (1961) 'What I see in the Maximus poems'. In Cook, J. (ed.) (2004) *Poetry in Theory: An anthology, 1900–2000*. Malden, MA: Blackwell Publishing.

Fenton, J. (2002) *An Introduction to English Poetry*. London: Viking.

Gagné, R. (1970) *The Conditions of Learning*, 2nd edn. London: Holt, Rinehart and Winston.

Gardner, H. (2011) *Frames of Mind: The theory of multiple intelligences*. New York: Basic Books.

Gibson, R. (1998) *Teaching Shakespeare*. Cambridge: Cambridge University Press.

Guppy, P. and Hughes, M. (1999) *The Development of Independent Reading: Reading support explained*. Buckingham: Open University Press.

HMI (1987) *Teaching Poetry in the Secondary School: An HMI view*. London: HMSO.

Hoyles, A. and Hoyles, M. (2000) *Moving Voices: Black performance poetry*. London: Hansib.

Hughes, T. (1967) *Poetry in the Making: An anthology of poems and programmes from 'Listening and Writing'*. London: Faber and Faber.

Hyland, P. (1992) *Getting into Poetry: A readers' and writers' guide to the poetry scene*. Newcastle-upon-Tyne: Bloodaxe.

Illeris, K. (2007) *How We Learn: Learning and non-learning in school and beyond*. London: Routledge.

Johnson, S. (2005) *Everything Bad is Good for You: How today's popular culture is actually making us smarter*. London: Riverhead Books.

Krathwohl, D., Bloom, B., and Masia, B. (1971) *Taxonomy of Educational Objectives: Handbook 2, Affective domain*. London: Longman Group.

Kress, G.R. (2003) *Literacy in the New Media Age*. London: Routledge.

Kress, G. and Van Leeuwen, T. (2001) *Multimodal Discourse: The modes and media of contemporary communication*. London: Arnold.

MacDonagh, T. (1920?) *The Death Speech of Thomas MacDonagh, Irish Patriot*. Undated. New Haven, CT: Brick Row Print and Book Shop.

Matthewman, S. (2011) *Teaching Secondary English as if the Planet Matters*. London: Routledge.

Meek, M., Warlow, A., and Barton, G. (eds) (1977) *The Cool Web: The pattern of children's reading*. London: The Bodley Head.

Ofsted (2007) *Poetry in Schools: A survey of practice, 2006/07*. London: Ofsted.

Ong, W. (1982) *Orality and Literacy: The technologizing of the word*. London: Methuen.

Padel, R. (2004) *52 Ways of Looking at a Poem: Or, how reading modern poetry can change your life*. London: Vintage.

Paterson, D. (ed.) (1999) *101 Sonnets: From Shakespeare to Heaney*. London: Faber and Faber.

Pearse, P. (1966) *Plays, Stories, Poems*. Dublin: Talbot Press.

Piaget, J. (2001) *The Psychology of Intelligence*. Translated by Piercy, M. and Berlyne, D.E. London: Routledge.

Rosen, M. (2007) *Poetry Basics*. Online. www.videojug.com/interview/poetry-basics-2

Rosenblatt, L.M. (1978) *The Reader, the Text, the Poem: The transactional theory of the literary work*. Carbondale, IL: Southern Illinois University Press.

Ryan, D. (1979) *The 1916 Poets*. Westport, CT: Greenwood Press.

Segall, A. (2004) 'Revisiting pedagogical content knowledge: The pedagogy of content/the content of pedagogy'. *Teaching and Teacher Education*, 20: 489–504.

Smythe, C. (1995) *A Guide to Coole Park: Home of Lady Gregory*. Gerrards Cross, Buckinghamshire: Colin Smythe.

Tsui, A.B.M. (2005) 'Expertise in teaching: Perspectives and issues'. In Johnson, K. (ed.) *Expertise in Second Language Learning and Teaching*. Basingstoke, Hampshire: Palgrave Macmillan.

Vygotsky, L. (1986) *Thought and Language*, revised edn. Cambridge, MA: MIT Press.

Wallace, J. (2013) Songwriting Survey: 'What do you think are the differences between a poem and a song lyric?' Online. www.musesmuse.com/poem-vs-lyric.html

Wood, J. and Wood, L. (1995) *Cambridge Critical Workshop*. Cambridge: Cambridge University Press.

Yeats reference list

Ellmann, R. (1961) *Yeats: The man and the masks*. London: Faber and Faber.

— (1964) *The Identity of Yeats*. London: Faber and Faber.

Foster, R.F. (1998) *W.B. Yeats, A Life: I, The apprentice mage 1865–1914*. Oxford: Oxford University Press.

— (2003) *W.B. Yeats, A Life: II, The arch-poet 1915–1939*. Oxford: Oxford University Press.

National Library of Ireland Online Yeats Exhibition www.nli.ie/yeats

Yeats, W.B. (1990) *Collected Poems*. London: Picador.

— (1990) *A Vision and Related Writings*. London: Arena.

Index